Praise for *Read the Bible like a Mystic*

"Carl McColman writes from a heart transformed by mystical love and invites the reader onto a powerful journey of seeing Scripture in new ways. What a gift this book is, to help save the ancient texts sacred to Christian and Jewish traditions from fundamentalist agendas, and to invite us into ways of reading that are spacious, imaginative, full of mystery and wonder, and overflowing with deepened love and transformation. Carl gives his readers a generous map to the heart of wisdom through imaginative encounters with the sacred texts. Highly recommended reading for all contemplatives."

—**Christine Valters Paintner**, PhD, online abbess of Abbey of the Arts and author of more than twenty books on the contemplative path

"Read the Bible like a Mystic is a refreshing book that allows readers to find the pearls of wisdom hidden in the biblical stories. Carl McColman's mysticism of the ordinary invites the reader to approach the biblical stories as a contemplative so as to discover the awe and wonder of God as Infinite Love."

—**Dr. Cristóbal Serrán-Pagán y Fuentes**, assistant professor of philosophy of religion at Palacký University, Czech Republic, and editor of *Merton and the Tao*

"Some read the Bible thinking it's a menu. Mystics read the Bible knowing it's the meal: internalizing its wisdom and making it a part of their being and becoming. Carl McColman's *Read the Bible like a Mystic* is a powerful invitation to pick up the Bible and "come and eat" (John 21:12). I hope you are brave enough to accept it."

—**Rabbi Rami Shapiro**, author of *Perennial Wisdom for the Spiritually Independent*

"In this urgently needed book, Carl McColman gets straight to the point: The conventional sales pitches for why the Bible should (or should not) matter no longer work. In a world where we have a rational explanation for almost everything but yearn for meaning, the Bible's potential for individual and cultural renewal must lie in the realm of imagination, mystery, and mysticism. Turns out, this was the Bible's domain all along! *Read the Bible like a Mystic* will help you see what has always been hiding in plain sight. Get ready for an infusion of beauty, wonder, and meaning that you won't be able to unsee!"

—**Heather Hamilton**, author of *Returning to Eden: A Field Guide to the Spiritual Journey*

"Read the Bible like a Mystic is for anyone who has ever felt astonished, mystified, or frustrated by Christian Scripture. Particularly for those who've known the pain of Scripture weaponized against them, and for those who've attempted to make

sense of its complexities, but experienced a mix of headache, disagreement, longing, and wonder, Carl McColman's wise book is an honest, helpful guide. It acknowledges this ancient text as imperfect. It invites us to enter it as a kaleidoscopic conversation that includes puzzling and problematic passages plus sage and sublime poetry and prose singing of cosmic love for earth and all creatures on it. Into this centuries-old mess and gorgeousness, Carl brings a trusted, intelligent, kind, and down-to-earth questioning. He approaches this revered religious bestseller in the humble spirit of interdependence with earth and with local-and-global communities in need of neighborliness, equity, and justice. His book is itself a dialogue about actually reading and engaging with the Bible, not literally, nor shallowly, but contemplatively. We're invited to explore a mystical sensibility that opens to new possibilities in our relationship with this enduring anthology. Carl's book is a valuable conversation starter for us all!"

—**Carmen Acevedo Butcher**, PhD, poet and award-winning translator of *The Cloud of Unknowing*, *Practice of the Presence* by Brother Lawrence, and Hildegard of Bingen

"Carl McColman's *Read the Bible like a Mystic* is a vital guide for those seeking a deeper, more transformative relationship with Scripture. In a time when the Bible is often misused to divide, oppress, and harm, McColman invites us to rediscover its power as a source of justice and profound spiritual wisdom.

This book is a must-read for anyone yearning to engage the sacred text with fresh eyes and a contemplative heart."

—**Brandan Robertson**, pastor and author of *Queer & Christian: Reclaiming the Bible, Our Faith, and Our Place at the Table*

"In these times of fear and exile, we are grasping for wisdom to survive. When our terror and alienation get projected onto the Bible, we sadly distort the wisdom we are desperately reaching for. Carl McColman, in this book, is offering us an invitation and instructions on how to pause and reorient our minds and hearts toward mystery and wholeness—mystic consciousness—so that we may truly discover the wisdom we seek in the Bible and experience the heaven on earth we can create."

—**Pamela Ayo Yetunde**, ThD, pastoral counselor and author of *Casting Indra's Net* and *Dearly Beloved: Prince, Spirituality, and This Thing Called Life*

"With *Read the Bible like a Mystic*, Carl McColman does something beautiful: He helps us reflect on the potential to transform the way we appreciate the Bible, so we can actually appreciate our own complex lives more and rest in the abiding presence of God that soaks us all with love. Above all, this is a book that helps me breathe."

—**Stuart Higginbotham**, Episcopal priest, assistant professor in the practice of spiritual formation and ministry, Candler School of Theology at Emory University, and author of *The Heart of a Calling* and *Bones of Light: Poems of Spiritual Imagination*

"If you've been hankering for a deeper engagement with the Bible but find yourself put off by the heavy-handed ways in which its teaching is so often delivered these days, Carl McColman proposes a refreshing alternative: Why not learn to read the Bible like a mystic? In this delightful, non-technical book, he lets you in on an open secret known to Christian monks and mystics for nearly two thousand years: that reading the Bible is not about dogma and certainty; it's an open-ended engagement with the Infinite, which calls on the best of your own creativity and spiritual imagination and prizes the unique authority of your own experience. Drawing on the lives of mystics both ancient and contemporary, he shows you how this engagement works and the surprising places it can lead you if you're willing to take it seriously and work at it patiently."

—**Cynthia Bourgeault**, author of *The Wisdom Way of Knowing* and *The Wisdom Jesus*

"Carl McColman asks if the Bible can be saved—saved, that is, from the dead literalism that prevails today. His answer is a powerful and resounding yes. No one should presume to assert what the Bible says or does not say without understanding the truths that McColman presents here. This book is urgently needed."

—**Richard Smoley**, author of *Inner Christianity: A Guide to the Esoteric Tradition*

"There are a lot of reasons mystical theology and biblical theology have parted company in the last five hundred years. In this simple but profound book written for the layperson, Carl McColman makes a compelling case for bringing them back together. At the heart of biblical theology is an encounter with the living God. The same is true of the heart of mystical theology. Despite all the ways the Bible has been used and misused, can we again bring that encounter to our reading? McColman shows us how. This book will expand your imagination, give you new ways to read the Bible, return you to old stories, and introduce you to unexpected companions."

—**Amy Frykholm**, author of *Julian of Norwich: A Contemplative Biography* and *Christian Understandings of the Future*

"Carl McColman's *Read the Bible like a Mystic* doesn't shy away from the hard parts of the text, nor does it excuse them away. Instead he invites us into a new way of reading: one less focused on historicity and doctrine and more focused on connecting to the heart of the Divine. For those who have been hurt by the Bible, for those who find it confusing or outdated, for those who used to read it and are longing to find a way back in, this book is for you. This is an invitation to read with the heart, in the tradition of the many Christian mystics. Accessible, invitational, and filled with wisdom, this is a guide to reading in a new way."

—**Shannon T. L. Kearns**, author of *No One Taught Me How to Be a Man: What a Trans Man's Experience Reveals about Masculinity* and co-founder of queertheology.com

"*Read the Bible like a Mystic* offers a renewed approach to reading the Bible that is invitational and freeing, and allows for the truth of our own lives to flourish. Carl McColman offers us a way to shake up the status quo and transcend our preconceived notions about the Bible, all while bringing us back to the root of Christianity."

—**Cassidy Hall**, author of *Queering Contemplation: Finding Queerness in the Roots and Future of Contemplative Spirituality*

"Carl McColman has written this treasure of a book "in the fullness of time" as many spiritual seekers today long for a deeper, more authentic sense of the Spirit in their daily lives. *Read the Bible like a Mystic* spotlights luminous not-to-be-missed passages of the Bible that, together with Carl's expert and insightful guidance, serve as holy reminders to us that the infinite spirit of God within and all around us can be discovered, encountered, and intimately known when we engage certain sacred texts of Scripture with a mystic's "listening heart and wondering mind." This must-read book will be an always-at-your-side resource that you will recommend to your friends who are just beginning their spiritual journey, as well as to those with years devoted to the richness and power of Scripture. It is that eye-opening!"

—**Caroline Oakes**, author of *Practice the Pause: Jesus' Contemplative Practice, New Brain Science, and What It Means to Be Fully Human*

"Carl McColman's latest book, *Read the Bible like a Mystic*, is a stirring invitation to embrace the Bible as a book of wisdom. With great candor and courage, he suggests that we abandon the literal reading of fundamentalists, retain the important but limited reading of academic scholars, and move beyond both to embrace a contemplative reading of the Bible that allows for mystery and unknowing. Just as the practice of meditation and contemplation can expand the heart and mind, so too can this book. McColman's extensive and personal experience, combined with his approachable writing style, has produced a truly inspired work. This is an important book for the current spiritual climate, and I highly recommend it for contemplatives everywhere."

—**Mark Dannenfelser**, founding director of the Mindfulness Center of Atlanta and cohost of the *Opening Minds, Opening Hearts* podcast produced by Contemplative Outreach International

READ
THE **BIBLE**
LIKE A
MYSTIC

READ
THE BIBLE
LIKE A
MYSTIC

Contemplative Wisdom
and the Word

CARL McCOLMAN

Broadleaf Books
Minneapolis

READ THE BIBLE LIKE A MYSTIC
Contemplative Wisdom and the Word

30 29 28 27 26 25 24   1 2 3 4 5 6 7 8 9

Unless noted otherwise, scripture quotations are from the New Revised Standard
Version Bible, © 1989, Division of Christian Education of the National Council
of the Churches of Christ in the United States of America. Used by permission.
All rights reserved.

Library of Congress Control Number: 2024034532 (print)

Cover image © 2024 Getty Images; Clearing clouds/1043299678 by Paul Taylor
Cover design by Broadleaf Books

Print ISBN: 978-1-5064-8630-7
eBook ISBN: 978-1-5064-8631-4

Printed in India.

For Cynthia and Margaret

CONTENTS

For one word of [the Bible] will contain within itself a thousand mysteries, and thus our understanding is only very elementary.

—Saint Teresa of Ávila

*   *   *

1

Michelangelo's Statue

Whether it's the Bible or the Qur'an, the mystics have never found God by reading about God. There is no class, no lecture, no homily that will ever bring you closer to God. Because there is, in fact, absolutely nothing you could ever learn about God. For the mystics, the only way to know God is to experience God. And the only way to experience God is to unlearn everything the ego has been trying so vigorously to manufacture since our infancy.

—Brian C. Muraresku

*   *   *

IF YOU LONG for a deeper, more contemplative, more mystical relationship with the unnameable mystery we call God, then read the Bible like a mystic: like someone whose life has been illuminated and transformed by immersion in the very heart of divine love. Read from the heart of compassionate love, not from fear or any anxious need to please, placate, or control.

If you want to have a meaningful relationship with the wisdom teachings of Jesus, especially to have those teachings liberated from all the ways that institutional religious Christianity has distorted, misunderstood, or weaponized those teachings in the service of power and authority, then read the Bible like a mystic, for a mystical reading of Scripture can be a way for you to reconnect with the uncreated light that shines at the heart of those ancient words of wisdom and love.

*   *   *

When Michelangelo carved his iconic statue of David, the story goes that he simply found a suitable slab of marble and then proceeded to carve away every bit of rock that wasn't part of David. By that process of elimination, one of the great works of Renaissance art came into being.

Mysticism, in a similar way, has long held that one of the most helpful and authentic ways to talk about God is to begin by talking about what God is not. After all, who is truly qualified to say anything about God? (Perhaps the people who insist that they have all the answers are the *least* qualified!) Whatever we mean by *God*, we are speaking of something or someone that is ultimately a mystery—and part of the mysteriousness of God is the simple fact that we cannot capture God in the limited field of human language and thought. If we cannot ever adequately say what God *is*, perhaps we need to approach this unspeakable topic merely by seeking to say what God is *not*.

Over the years I have come to believe that, at least as far as Christian mysticism is concerned, one cannot truly know the way of the (Christian) mystic without also knowing the wisdom of the Bible. But the more I reflected on that principle, the more I have come to believe that the inverse is equally true: to truly unlock the mysteries of the Bible, we need to approach Scripture not with the literalism of a fundamentalist, the derision of an atheist, or even just the skepticism of a scholar but with the visionary, unknowing wonder of a mystic.

When I sat down to write this book, I realized that it is an impossible book to write. At least, it is an impossible book for *me* to write. Like many people who have drunk from the well of the mystics, I am much more conscious of how much I *don't* know about mystical theology or contemplative philosophy—let alone biblical scholarship. Many years have passed since I gave up on the naive, literalistic faith of fundamentalists, and I do not have the academic training of Bible commentators. I am uncomfortable with the sardonic cynicism that has become the fashionable stance of the agnostics and atheists of our time: the scoffing idea that we have no idea if God, or even truth and beauty and goodness, exists, so why bother talking or writing about such things? I have no credentials or qualifications to write this or any book about the Bible—other than the fact that I have been reading the Bible for about half a century now, and like many people, I find it deeply inspiring, profoundly troubling, strangely beautiful, endlessly maddening, and expansively mysterious by turns. If the mystics have taught me anything, their diversity and candor encourage me to be fearlessly honest about the fact that the Bible seems to me to be a hot mess—one that helps us connect with the mystery we call *God* but a hot mess nevertheless.

So why did I write this book anyway? I have a couple of reasons.

I once heard a talk on public radio by Anne Lamott where she said she advised writers to write the book they wish they could read. If somebody had helped me connect the dots between mysticism and the Bible when I was a teenager or young adult, it might have saved me an untold amount of angst and years spent reading the Bible in the wrong way for the wrong reasons. So I'm writing this book in the hopes that it might be of some small help to someone else. I learned how to read the Bible like a mystic the hard way; maybe this book could save you from making some of the same mistakes I made.

My other inspiration comes from G. K. Chesterton's adage, "If a thing is worth doing, it is worth doing badly." Chesterton was a champion of the ordinary person who did something for love rather than for money. And while it is true that I will receive a modest royalty from the sales of this book, my relationship with the Bible is most definitely that of an amateur: I have no academic degree or other professional credentials to justify me as a scholar or an expert; all I stand on is my love for the book (a love that, as you will see, is fraught and troubled but love nonetheless). As an amateur, I am writing for other amateurs: people motivated to explore spirituality, mysticism, and the Bible not for professional standing or vocational ambition but simply as an expression of love: love for the Bible but, even more so, love for the mystery we call God and perhaps even simply love for life itself (a love that, I believe, is necessary for any truly healthy and meaningful spirituality).

While I do not deserve to compare my modest skills as a writer to Michelangelo's genius, I feel like the best way to begin this book is to follow in the great Renaissance artist's footsteps and carve away all the things that this book is not. In our exploration of what it means to read the Bible like a mystic, here are a few things that I am *not* doing. This is not an academic or scholarly book; I'm writing strictly from a spiritual perspective. Biblical scholarship—the rarefied study of the Bible and its meaning, which takes place primarily at universities and other institutions of higher learning—is critically important for an intelligent and honest understanding of the Bible and its place in our society. The Bible is a badly abused book, and much of the abuse of that book comes at the hands of religious functionaries who often willfully ignore the work of Bible scholars, historians, and other academics who have devoted their lives to understanding and interpreting the history of the Bible and of how it has been interpreted and understood over the centuries. In our legal system, we hold the principle that ignorance of the law is no excuse—if you are arrested for a crime, you cannot simply tell the judge you must be innocent because you had no idea that what you did was wrong. Likewise, trying to interpret the Bible without at least a layperson's knowledge of Scripture scholarship and critical interpretation is spiritually irresponsible, whether you think so or not. It's a display not of *faith* but of *ignorance*, and it's high time we stop confusing the two. So while this is not a scholarly book, I want to be clear that I believe becoming familiar with biblical scholarship is essential to read the Bible not only like a mystic but also responsibly.

Although it's necessary, scholarship also has its limits. Theory needs practice to be relevant to the real world. You could devote a lifetime to studying human sexuality and read all the most learned writings on the topic (here's looking at you, Masters and Johnson), but if you do not actually make yourself vulnerable and available for a kind and loving and intimate relationship with another person, where the two of you both freely consent to unite in physical love, then you will never truly and fully understand sex. Likewise, the academic study of Scripture is not the same thing as a mystical reading of the Bible, and scholarship by itself will not be enough to read the Bible in a truly mystical and prayerful way, which means opening your heart to the encounter with the divine mystery that the Bible, at its best, invites us into.

Having said all that, my point is this: While I hope that what I write in this book is *informed by* and consistent with the best Bible scholarship, this is not, in itself, a book intended for scholars or meant as a contribution to biblical scholarship. Rather, I am writing for the ordinary reader, persons like you and me who seek to relate to the Bible in the light of our own personal and communal spiritual lives.

This is not a guide to specific teachings or doctrines based on the Bible; instead, I leave that for you to explore on your own when you read Scripture. People read the Bible for many reasons: to understand what the biblical writers had to say about God, or Jesus, or the Holy Spirit, or angels and life after death; to get a sense of Christian beliefs regarding morality, ethics, money, miracles, healing, justice, and other spiritual topics. Many Christians have been socialized to read the Bible in order to find out what it takes to be "saved"—even though, interestingly enough, not all Christians can even agree on what salvation means. And that right there is a hint as to why I'm avoiding discussions about doctrine, dogma, or theology. Not only do all the different Christian churches have widely divergent ways of understanding the message of the Bible, but even the Bible itself often speaks with multiple voices that either disagree with one another or at least provide different perspectives. The purpose of this book is to make a case for reading the Bible in a particular way—following the inspiration of great mystics and contemplatives. My hope is that the principles discussed in this book can equip you to read the Bible for yourself—and discover for yourself what it has to say about various topics.

This is not a Bible commentary; it is a general invitation to Bible reading rather than a verse-by-verse guide. The

Bible, as a collection of ancient texts from the Middle East written in a culture and languages that are foreign to most readers today, often seems mysterious and challenging when spiritual seekers first start to read it. The Bible was created communally (it was written, edited, and curated by dozens of mostly unknown contributors over many centuries), and so it needs to be interpreted communally as well. We need each other's insights, perspectives, experiences, and skills to fully understand what this ancient book is trying to tell us. This is why commentaries on the Bible are so helpful for readers. A good Bible commentary will guide you chapter by chapter or even verse by verse through Scripture. That's not what this book is trying to do, however: I'm looking at the Bible and mystical spirituality from more of a big-picture perspective. The Bible is not a monoculture; it is an ecosystem—in other words, many different voices, perspectives, and even values all contribute to create the book we call the Bible, just like many different birds, frogs, and crickets combine to make the symphony of sound that we can encounter in nature. A good commentary can help you recognize all those different voices (or species, to continue with the ecosystem metaphor). That's important work, but not what I'm trying to do here.

Like most people who have become interested in the Bible, I love good commentaries: books written by Bible experts and scholars to provide important background information and insights to unlock the mysteries of these ancient writings. Nowadays, you can find many different commentaries, often written from different perspectives (two of my favorites are *The Women's Bible Commentary* and *The Queer Bible Commentary*). The more of these you consult, the more well-rounded your appreciation of the Bible will be. I have long felt that there is a need for a *Contemplative Bible Commentary*—a curated book that brings together insights from contemplative practitioners who are also Bible scholars—to help illuminate the rich mystical and contemplative teachings that are often hidden in plain sight in the Bible text (e.g., some verses, like Psalm 65:1 or 1 Thessalonians 4:11, often convey a much more contemplative or even mystical sense in their original language than their English translation suggests). *Read the Bible like a Mystic*, however, is not a commentary like that, and I mention it in the hopes that a scholar/contemplative might someday work to create such a resource. A commentary like that would be a gift to the Christian faith and the human family, so if any contemplative-oriented Bible scholars are reading this, consider yourself invited to prayerfully consider whether such a book is in *your* future. Meanwhile, my hope for *this* book is more modest: rather than providing a verse-by-verse commentary on the Bible as a whole, I hope reading this book can invite you to bring your own mystical sensibility to the biblical ecosystem—and also to read, like a mystic, whichever commentaries you find helpful as you seek to know and understand the wisdom of Scripture.

This is not an introductory book on mysticism; rather, it is a meditation on how to bring mysticism and Scripture together. If you are new to mysticism, please read my previous work, *The New Big Book of Mysticism*; two other books worth checking out are Evelyn Underhill's *Mysticism* and John Mabry's *Growing into God*. These books will be a good start to get a sense of this big and beautiful topic. The great German theologian Karl Rahner famously said, "The Christian of the future will be a mystic or will not exist," and I, like many others of our generation, believe that mysticism is an essential key to any meaningful spirituality, Christian or otherwise. If you are brand new to mysticism, reading this book will give you plenty of insights into just what it is and why it matters, but it will be like joining in on an in-progress conversation at a party and having to pick up as you go along. You can do it, but if you take the time to read one or more introductory books, you'll get up to speed much more quickly.

This is not a collection of devotional or spiritual exercises; it is simply an invitation to a visionary relationship with the Bible. Given the topic I am exploring, when I started to write this book I was tempted to focus on Ignatian spirituality and *lectio divina*—two popular, Scripture-based approaches to contemplative prayer that fall squarely in the Christian contemplative/mystical tradition. But wonderful books on those foundational spiritual practices already exist (for *lectio divina*, check out *Sacred Reading* by Michael Casey or *Lectio Divina* by Christine Valters Paintner; for Ignatian prayer, read *Inner Compass* by Margaret Silf or *An Ignatian*

Introduction to Prayer by Timothy Gallagher), so I didn't see the point in reinventing the wheel. This book is more of a *why* than a *how* kind of book: I'd like to invite you into the conversation of *why* it matters to read the Bible like a mystic, and I encourage you to follow up with folks like Michael Casey or Margaret Silf to get a better grounding in different approaches of *how* to do that.

Nevertheless, if you'd like a brief introduction to *lectio divina* or Ignatian prayer, see the appendix of this book, where I offer concise overviews of those ancient disciplines for reading the Bible in a prayerful way.

*   *   *

Many mystics go to great lengths to declare what God is not, but at the end of the day, does this get us any closer to understanding what the mystery of God really is? It's a question that is very much open for debate. For now, let's join in on the adventure of trying to explore that unsayable mystery—the mystery of God—by looking at the Bible, Western culture's foundational document about God, and how people have related to God and one another in God. Reading the Bible like a mystic does not guarantee us a mystical experience of God. But it has been said that enlightenment is an accident, so meditation and other spiritual practices are worthwhile because they make us accident-prone. If a conscious mystical experience of God is likewise an unpredictable possibility, then reading the Bible—especially reading it as a mystic would—might just be a way of making ourselves available for that uncontrollable, life-transforming moment.

The Bible is an amazing book. It's a literary masterpiece, a theological treasure trove, and a powerful resource for an ever-deepening mystical spirituality. It is also a difficult book that has been terribly abused and misunderstood and has been weaponized by people who think spirituality is about control rather than compassion. I hope this modest little exploration of how to approach the Bible with the heart of a mystic and the insight of a contemplative will not only help you have a positive and affirming understanding of the Bible but also equip you to recognize when someone is misusing the Bible. May we all use Scripture only to dive more deeply into the infinite heart of infinite love; then we truly will read the Bible like mystics.

Many people approach the Bible in different ways (in chapter 4, we'll look at four common approaches to reading Scripture). There are many ideas and teachings surrounding the Bible: it has been called the word of God, the only essential spiritual resource ("Holy Scripture containeth all things necessary for salvation"), and the ultimate authority on spiritual matters. Think of all the ways that people talk *about* the Bible as being like clothing on a body. Perhaps to read the Bible like a mystic, we need to undress this body and just be present with its vulnerable beauty. Like Michelangelo removing the unnecessary pieces of rock from his statue, we can remove all the unnecessary "clothing" that hides us from the naked words of this ancient spiritual text. The famous Zen teacher Shunryu Suzuki taught the concept of "beginner's mind," suggesting that to practice Zen we have to let go of all our preconceived notions and learn to meditate with the innocence of a beginner—even if we've been studying meditation for many years. Let's undress the Bible with a similar beginner's mind: let go of any preconceived notions you have about what the Bible might mean (or doesn't mean) and approach it with the open mind of a true beginner. That might very well be the first step to reading Scripture like a mystic.

But first, perhaps we need to address one very big elephant in the room: While some people have dressed up the Bible with a lot of ideas about it being the inerrant word of God, others have covered it over with a cloak of shame, insisting that because it contains passages that appear to condone violence, slavery, sexism, and homophobia, there's no point in reading it at all. When we undress the Bible, we need to reckon with both of these "fashions," and so that is the subject to which we first must turn.

*   *   *

2

Can the Bible Be Saved?

I asked [my grandmother] one day why it was that she would not let me read any of the Pauline letters. What she told me I shall never forget. "During the days of slavery," she said, "the master's minister would occasionally hold services for the slaves. Old man McGhee was so mean that he would not let a Negro minister preach to his slaves. Always the white minister used as his text something from Paul. At least three or four times a year he used as a text: 'Slaves, be obedient to them that are your masters . . . , as unto Christ.' Then he would go on to show how it was God's will that we were slaves and how, if we were good and happy slaves, God would bless us. I promised my Maker that if I ever learned to read and if freedom ever came, I would not read that part of the Bible."

—Howard Thurman

* * *

BEFORE WE CONSIDER what it means to read the Bible like a mystic, first we need to acknowledge that many people may not see the point of a book like this at all.

I can imagine many people, especially practicing Christians, would ask, "Why would I want to read the Bible like a *mystic*? I just want to read the Bible like a *believer*." Ever since my first book on Christian mysticism was published in 2010, I've been surprised at how many Christians seem to be either uninterested in or perhaps even slightly intimidated by or afraid of mysticism. They're interested in the Bible, naturally, but not in mysticism.

Meanwhile, plenty of other people seem to be coming from the opposite direction. They are interested in mysticism, all right: they might describe themselves as "spiritual but not religious." Mysticism sounds fascinating and intriguing—a doorway into a deeper and more meaningful spiritual life. Who wouldn't want that? But when it comes to the Bible, these people often are aware of passages in the Bible that have been used to harm people—passages that glorify violence and war—or that have been used to condone slavery, racism, the subjugation of women, and the oppression of queer people. These people would say, "The Bible? Sorry, I have no use for such a primitive and exclusionary book." They are interested in mysticism but not in the Bible.

Everyone is entitled to their way of thinking, of course, but I can't help but notice that for many people, the words *Bible* and *mystic* just don't seem to belong together. Chances are many people have a bad impression of one or the other. Somewhere along the way, they have learned to reject either mysticism or Scripture (or both).

So who is this book for? Well, if you've read this far, I hope it's for you. I imagine that readers of this book are probably interested in spirituality, which includes a recognition that the Bible is a sacred book to over a billion people on earth and also an understanding that mysticism is a concept that represents a deep and transformational spirituality that is at the core of every religion, and perhaps even transcends all the boundaries that separate religions and spiritual traditions from each other. I imagine that readers of this book are looking for a new way to approach the Bible and therefore are willing to give mysticism a try. One of my goals in writing this book is to make the case that a *mystical* approach to the Bible matters. In other words, learning to read the Bible like a mystic can help us find real spiritual meaning and wisdom for our times—present-day wisdom accessed through this ancient text.

*   *   *

But before we can truly appreciate a *mystical* way of reading the Bible, I feel like I need to acknowledge that many people in our time no longer see the value of *the Bible* itself. And frankly, I believe this is because the Bible is too easily misunderstood when it is read from the perspective of either true believers or true nonbelievers (i.e., fundamentalists or atheists).

To put this problem as bluntly as possible, Can the Bible itself be saved?

I'm not talking about saved in the conservative evangelical sense, as in "saved from hell." I'm asking if it's worth it to go to the trouble of learning how to read the Bible like a mystic, given that so many people (including many Christians) see the Bible as so ancient, so culturally limited, so patriarchal and homophobic, and so limited in how it depicts spirituality that it is no longer truly useful for spiritual seekers today.

*   *   *

Let's also acknowledge that many conservative Christians would be appalled at what I have just written. Especially if they are affiliated with more traditional churches or live in places where conservative ideology is dominant, many Christians treat the Bible with profound reverence, regarding it as truly sacred because they regard it as the word of God. When Christians feel this way about the Bible, naturally they believe it should be carefully studied, interpreted in accordance with traditional teachings, and, most important of all, obeyed— but never criticized, questioned, or doubted.

Meanwhile, people who do not share such a reverence for the Bible oftentimes have a very different understanding of the book. Instead of seeing it as the word of God, they are more likely to see it as no better or worse than any other ancient spiritual book. Many nonbelievers actually think of the Bible as dangerous—an ancient text that has been weaponized to promote a narrow, patriarchal, and frightening vision of society where non-Christians are seen as condemned by God; where women are clearly meant to be subservient to men, responsible only for homemaking and child-rearing and submissive to her husband's or father's role as "head" of the family; and where queer people are, at best, ignored and, at worst, regarded as immoral, sinful, mentally ill, or even criminal. And if all that weren't bad enough, it seems that far too many Christians simply ignore so many of the significant issues of our time, from economic inequality to climate change to racism and other forms of social privilege, because such issues are either not addressed in the Bible or not addressed in a way that fits in with their authoritarian worldview.

Is the Bible a book of spiritual wisdom and guidance, or is it a relic of ancient superstition, poorly equipped to meet the challenging issues of our time? This seems to be the first question we need to wrestle with.

Is the Bible a book that reveals the secrets of God and angels, of the meaning of life, and of what we can realistically hope for after we die? Or is it simply a record of obsolete beliefs, folktales, and legends that no longer make sense in the light of modern science, technology, psychology, and sociology?

Does the Bible provide a reliable roadmap for morality and ethics, or is it a problematic book containing too many passages that have been used by people with power to harm or oppress others?

*   *   *

Everybody will answer these questions differently. I encourage you to consider where your sympathies lie. Perhaps you believe that the Bible is the inerrant word of God, and it bothers you that people criticize it and question it as much as they do. Or perhaps you are the type of person who *does* question the claims that some religious people make about the Bible—after all, if it really is a supernatural book, then it should prove itself to be *better* than other books that make no claim to spiritual authority, so therefore it ought to be examined critically.

But no matter what your own thoughts may be, there's no denying that even a superficial critical examination of the Bible leads to a plethora of big questions.

*   *   *

The Bible is a book of myths. In other words, it relies on stories, rather than history or science, to explain why the world even exists or why people suffer and die or why men have historically wielded power and privilege over women. As ancient as the Bible is, its writers did not have access to our knowledge of physics or technology, of psychology and sociology, of sexuality and gender, or of cultural studies or conflict management, so we can't expect the Bible to speak with the same understanding that we take for granted in today's world—at least on any issue that requires that kind of knowledge. It is a book of ancient stories, and so the perspective it provides is, likewise, ancient (some would say *obsolete*).

*   *   *

Nevertheless, there's the long-standing belief, shared by many Christians, about this book being directly inspired by God. If it *is* the word of God, we should just obey it, no questions asked, right? Well, it's not that simple, even for many faithful Christians. Alternatively, when we recognize that the Bible represents a premodern, prescientific way of understanding humanity and the world, should we just throw it out altogether? But then what about the passages that shimmer with poetic beauty or that speak of justice, mercy, divine love, and forgiveness? Are we prepared to throw out the baby of spiritual wisdom along with the bathwater of its patriarchal, premodern worldview?

*   *   *

Even if you are a believer in God and Christ, I hope you understand how important it is to recognize that the Bible's way of explaining things just doesn't seem to hold water for most people alive today, who are accustomed to looking at the world through the eyes of science, psychology, and other evidence-based ways of understanding and knowing how the world works. For many people who hold a scientific worldview, the Bible seems at best quaint and naive; at worst, it seems positively harmful, contributing to human suffering rather than alleviating it.

*   *   *

The Bible is not the only ancient text that people turn to for guidance or inspiration. Every major religion has its share of myths and folktales to explain the creation of the world, why suffering exists, or what people ought to do to grow spiritually and live happy lives. Why should we assume that the Bible contains the unquestionable word of God, while every other text regarded as sacred around the world must therefore be erroneous? Isn't that just a type of cultural narcissism?

*   *   *

The Problem with the Bible

The main problem with the Bible is not just that it is a collection of ancient myths or even that it puts forth ideas that many people would now find objectionable. The main problem with the Bible is that too many people ignore how difficult it is for many others to believe the Bible, and instead these true believers insist that it must be accepted as literally true and beyond all questioning—and that their way of understanding the Bible should define society as a whole, not just for Christians but for all people. In many parts of the world, those people wield incredible social, economic, and political power, and their influence—sometimes in dominating, controlling, or authoritarian ways—can make life really difficult, if not dangerous, for people who do not adhere to, or fit neatly into, their narrow worldview.

*   *   *

The Bible is simply a book—a collection of stories, poems, and ideas. To say the Bible is dangerous is really to comment on how the Bible gets used, and abused, and weaponized by people who insist on reading it in a simplistically literalist, patriarchal, authoritarian, or controlling way. The problem is a problem of *power*—is the Bible a tool for people with social or religious power to control the lives of others, or is it a book meant to be of service to all people, not just those who fit into a narrow understanding of goodness or righteousness?

*   *   *

Perhaps the best strategy for fighting against the abuse and weaponization of the Bible is not simply to dismiss it as irrelevant or try to ignore it (that just leaves it in the hands of the fundamentalists) or to bury it under the scholarly intellectualization of Bible scholars (who write for each other and whose ideas are too often seen as irrelevant by ordinary Christians). Rather, the best way to combat the weaponization of the Bible is to recover an ancient way of reading the Bible, not as a blueprint for a specific social or political agenda but as a mystical and contemplative guidebook for spiritual wisdom and a spiritually grounded message of justice and inclusion. What I am describing here is an ancient approach to reading the Bible, but it pairs well with the realities of life today. Such an approach does not have to conflict with contemporary science and knowledge but seeks to integrate mystical wisdom with practical approaches to creating a better life for all people.

Why Some People Think the Bible Is Dangerous

If you are not familiar with the Bible or if your exposure to the Bible has mostly been filtered through the kind of churches that tend to put Scripture on a pedestal, you may not even recognize why the book is seen as so problematic by many nonbelievers or liberal Christians. So let's look at just a few verses that really sum up what's seen as *wrong* with the Bible. We'll start with one of the most notorious passages in the New Testament, Ephesians 5:22–24: "Wives, be subject to your husbands as you are to the Lord. For the husband is the head of the wife just as Christ is the head of the church, the body of which he is the Savior. Just as the church is subject to Christ, so also wives ought to be, in everything, to their husbands."

This is just one of the many passages in the Bible that enforce a rigid understanding of gender, paired with a clear sense that women should be submissive to men. It's a viewpoint that completely ignores the legacy of rape culture and violence against women and that dismisses literally half of the human race as undeserving of full freedom and autonomy.

It's bad enough that the Bible promotes gender inequality, but it also makes life difficult for LGBTQ people:

> *For this reason God gave them up to degrading passions. Their women exchanged natural intercourse for unnatural, and in the same way also the men, giving up natural intercourse with women, were consumed with passion for one another. Men committed shameless acts with men and received in their own persons the due penalty for their error. And since they did not see fit to acknowledge God, God gave them up to a debased mind and to things that should not be done. . . . They know God's decree, that those who practice such things deserve to die—yet they not only do them but even applaud others who practice them. (Romans 1:26–28, 32)*

There are only a small number of verses in the Bible that have been used to denounce same-sex attraction, but Christians who hate queer people get plenty of ammunition from just a few passages like this one. Many scholars today believe that the author of this passage was really trying to criticize lustful behavior rather than loving relationships, but that nuance does not show up in the passage, making it hard for ordinary readers to see this quotation as anything other than homophobic.

The scapegoating of women and queer people is part of an even larger problem in the Bible: it is far too easy to read Scripture as condoning violence and, in particular, war—it seems that the Bible maintains a simplistic morality of "if it's good for our side, it's okay"—while seemingly oblivious to the profound horrors of political and military violence. As 1 Samuel 15:2–3 states, "Thus says the Lord of hosts: I will punish the Amalekites for what they did in opposing the Israelites when they came up out of Egypt. Now go and attack Amalek and utterly destroy all that they have; do not spare them, but kill both man and woman, child and infant, ox and sheep, camel and donkey."

Is God a supernatural bully who takes sides in war and even promotes genocide? This passage sure makes it seem that way. I, for one, am not interested in worshipping a God who demands the utter destruction of those who oppose him. Is that a god or a monster?

But the aggression that is tolerated in the Bible isn't just on the level of nations at war; it also accepts the horror of slavery, where oppression takes place on a person-to-person and systemic level: "Slaves, submit yourselves to your masters with all respect, not only to the good and gentle but also to the cruel" (1 Peter 2:18). Is this *really* what God wants? Or is it what people with power want? Is this an expression of spiritual wisdom or authoritarian control? When Peter (or whoever the author was) dared to tell slaves to be obedient even to cruel masters, did he intend to say that slave owners get a free pass to treat the people they oppress any way they want? Take your pick, but either the author or God (or both) ends up looking bad here.

The same is true for the following quote: "Whoever comes to me and does not hate father and mother, wife and children, brothers and sisters, yes, and even life itself, cannot be my disciple" (Luke 14:26). This passage is quoting Jesus himself, whom Christians proclaim is the Son of God. Elsewhere the Bible says that God is love—but if that is so, how could the Son of a loving God so blithely instruct his followers to hate their family members? This makes even Jesus seem to have a shadow side. And unfortunately, it's not an isolated incident. Another passage recounts him cursing a fig tree simply because it didn't bear fruit when he was hungry (never mind that it wasn't even in season).

Scholars often try to explain away this passage by claiming that Jesus was speaking hyperbolically—in other words, using an extreme example to make a point. But this passage sounds just like the kind of things that authoritarian cult leaders say to their followers to exert complete control over them. If Jesus is the Son of God, shouldn't he be smart enough to find a far less aggressive way to make his point?

* * *

These are merely a handful of problematic passages—there are more where these came from. Some Christians insist that all the "bad" passages in the Bible are found in the

Old Testament, but please note that this is a terrible misunderstanding (and perhaps even subtly anti-Semitic since the Christian Old Testament is the Hebrew Scriptures, the Bible of the Jewish people). Note that all but one of these examples that I've provided to you come from the New Testament—the section of the Christian Bible that tells the story of Jesus and his earliest followers. When it comes to violence, slavery, patriarchy, and homophobia, it's sad but true to acknowledge that the Bible did *not* get better as the years passed.

*   *   *

Can the Bible Be Saved?

Passages like the ones above lead many reasonable readers to say, "No, the Bible is not valuable as a spiritual guidebook—it has too many problematic teachings." I understand that viewpoint. On the other hand, there is more to the Bible than its challenging passages. As troubling as they are (and as damaging as they have been in the hands of abusive and unloving Christians), the difficult verses still only represent a small percentage of the Bible's overall message. Just as a human being who is basically good and virtuous sometimes makes mistakes, even terrible mistakes, it's fair to say that the Bible can be seen as a basically wise and beautiful book that nevertheless has some real problems.

There is so much more to the Bible than just the problems detailed in this chapter. In writing this chapter, I considered creating an additional section to balance the difficult passages quoted above with some of the more beautiful, inspiring, or mystical passages in the Bible, but I decided not to do that because many of those passages are well-known to most Christians (and some will be featured throughout the chapters to come). The Bible contains some of the greatest spiritual writings of all time: the Beatitudes, where Jesus offers a beautiful vision of ethics based not on power but on humility and peacemaking; many of the psalms, ancient Hebrew poems and hymns that describe a God of great compassion and deep beauty; the love chapter of 1 Corinthians, which after almost two thousand years remains a profound and eloquent description of what love entails; the Song of Solomon, a joyous and frankly erotic description of the splendor of romantic love; and the list could go on. Numerous inspiring and beautiful passages grace the prophetic and wisdom writings of the Hebrew Scriptures, and many wondrous and insightful nuggets of wisdom and ethical teaching are found in pretty much every book of the Bible. I, for one, would consider it a tremendous loss if I never read the many luminous and love-infused passages of the Bible ever again simply because I could never find a way to make sense of its relatively small number of appalling verses (recognizing, of course, that those passages truly *are* appalling).

*   *   *

Yes, I believe the Bible can be "saved," or else I wouldn't be writing this book about it. But let's be clear: there is no point in trying to read the Bible like a mystic (or to read it at all) unless we are utterly and fearlessly honest about the fact that it contains too many passages that have been used to hurt people and are still being used to restrict people's freedom, tolerate injustice and oppression, and shore up social injustice.

The Bible was written communally, so we need to read it communally as well, which means we need to consider not only the viewpoint of people with power and authority (whether in biblical times or today), but we also need to read the text from the perspective of those who have too often been seen as outsiders or others—people who have been oppressed because of their gender, sexuality, or ethnicity; those who have been subjected to colonial rule (especially by Christians); or those who have been enslaved, rejected as sinful or immoral, or dismissed as foreigners or practitioners of foreign religions. If God is truly the God of all people, then the experiences and perspectives of all people must be considered when reading the Bible.

*   *   *

The necessary first step to truly save the Bible is, once and for all, to abandon the fundamentalist way of reading Scripture.

There is an old proverb attributed to the Quakers: "It is better to light a candle than to curse the darkness." With that in mind, I wish I didn't have to mention fundamentalism or religious authoritarianism at all in this book. But to light the candle for a mystical reading of the Bible, I must speak out against the blindness of biblical fundamentalism, which is the widespread tendency among many Christians to believe the Bible should be read simplistically and literally because it is seen as the inerrant word of an authoritarian God. According to a recent poll conducted by the Pew Research Center, 26 percent of American Catholics and 55 percent of Evangelical Protestants believe the Bible is the word of God and should be taken literally. More than half of the Christians who participated in this poll held that view. So even if you (the reader of this book) are not a fundamentalist yourself, you probably know plenty of fundamentalists, given how many Christians fall into that camp. Or perhaps you came out of a fundamentalist church and are now trying to find a new, healthier, and more responsible way to approach the Bible. I hope you find the mystical approach to Scripture to be healing and inspiring. "Mysticism is the antidote to fundamentalism," according to the psychedelic activist Rick Doblin, and I thoroughly agree with him.

Intellectual honesty and ethical integrity both require that we must let go of the idea that even the most outrageous verses in the Bible are authoritative and unquestionably the word of God. If the only way to approach the Bible is to insist that every single passage in it is the inerrant and literal word of God, then perhaps the Bible cannot be saved. But that's not the only way to approach the Bible—for the mystics can inspire us to read it in a way that is more honest, balanced, and consistent with the sum total of all human knowledge (including the wisdom that comes to us through other faiths, science, psychology, and sociology).

The question of how to read and interpret the Bible is a question of *exegesis*. That word is simply the Greek term for *explanation* or *interpretation*; Bible scholars and preachers recognize exegesis as encompassing the principles or methods used to interpret the Bible (or any text). For example, the fundamentalist approach to exegesis is based on an authoritarian, patriarchal, and hierarchical image of God; stresses the idea that the Bible ought to be read in a literalistic manner; insists that the Bible is *inerrant* (that there is no error in the Bible, making it a reliable document speaking for the will of this authoritarian God); and is insistent that there is only one correct interpretation of Scripture. Furthermore, "one correct interpretation" rejects any criticism of the Bible that is based on science or historical/critical Bible scholarship. By contrast, a mystical way of interpreting the Bible is egalitarian rather than hierarchical; sees God as infinitely loving and compassionate rather than patriarchal and authoritarian; is willing to read the Bible in the light of scholarship and other branches of knowledge; and, most important of all, humbly recognizes that the Bible can be interpreted in many ways.

* * *

Mystics from the earliest centuries of the Christian era have acknowledged that it is a mistake to only read the Bible in a literalistic way. When we read the Bible like the mystics, we trust the guidance of the Spirit in our own hearts, which gives us both the courage and the freedom to acknowledge that the Bible contains profound spiritual wisdom but also deserves to be criticized when it appears to promote violence, racism, sexism, homophobia, or any other -ism that is contrary to the compassion and mercy of God.

*   *   *

To read the Bible like a mystic means learning to read it in a complex and nuanced way. What authoritarian "true believers" and atheists have in common is that they read the Bible in a simplistic and one-dimensional fashion. The mystics offer us a different approach: letting the Bible simultaneously be a flawed work of human culture that deserves the same criticism as any other work of literature or art and also a precious record of how ancient people understood God and sought to live according to the beauty and freeing power of divine love. When we take this both/and approach to the Bible, we begin to read it like a mystic.

*   *   *

Fear, Power, and Truth

In her autobiography, the great Spanish mystic Teresa of Ávila offers this revealing confession: "Without a doubt, I fear those who fear the devil more than I fear the devil himself." Apply this line of thinking to the Bible, and one could say, "I do not struggle with the Bible nearly as much as I struggle with those who use their interpretation of the Bible to marginalize or exclude others."

The Bible is not only a book about God; it is also a book about humanity, and therefore it is a book about how human beings relate to one another—which means it is a book about power, control, and authority. Many of the biblical authors appear to accept some expressions of power that nearly all of us today find unacceptable, such as slavery or the subjugation of women. This understanding of power seems to be embedded in an assumption for at least some of the biblical writers that God is an authority figure who cannot be questioned. Meanwhile, other biblical voices *do* suggest that God can be questioned— Job being one well-known example. It's important to realize that the Bible contains many different ideas about God and therefore divergent ideas about humanity—including how we exercise power and control and authority in our social relationships. For example, the words of the prophets and other biblical figures directly challenge some power structures, such as the power that wealthy and privileged people sometimes try to wield over everyone else. Whether the Bible is addressing how humans relate to God or one another, the imperative of justice, or even how to manage the complexities of human gender and sexuality, a careful study of the many different voices and perspectives in the Bible reveals that Scripture does not speak with a single voice and often can be seen as challenging the status quo in surprising ways. The Bible can be read as a book that explores the ways human beings use religious authority, spirituality, and ordinary political power to dominate, exclude, or control each other—and it offers insights into how we can deconstruct those oppressive systems of power and chart a path toward the kind of society that Jesus and the prophets envisioned: a society of radical inclusivity and equality where liberating justice and equity take priority over systems of privilege and power that can oppress or enslave.

To read the Bible like a mystic doesn't mean we just ignore or discount the difficult or triggering passages (even though we must commit to never using them to cause harm). Rather, a mystical reading of the Bible sees it as a conversation with many voices chiming in. Unfortunately, some of those voices are racist, sexist, homophobic, classist, or comfortable with the authoritarian exercise of power. But other voices also present in the Bible seek to challenge all of the above, promoting a world where privilege is dismantled, nonviolence is an ethical mandate, and compassion is the guiding principle for both individual behavior and social norms. Learning to read the Bible like a mystic includes learning to recognize all those different voices and discern which ones primarily function as "bad" examples and which ones are truly there to inspire us and draw us closer to God. When we read the Bible to connect with those compassionate and just voices, it is not only the Bible that is saved, but we ourselves also become more whole.

* * *

3

Reclaiming the Mystical Heart of Scripture

Underneath all the moralizing and polemic in the New Testament, there is a message of divinization, theosis; that is to say, in the way appropriate to humans we may once again through grace, by our kenosis, our self-forgetfulness in our lived beholding, realize our glory, our shared nature with God that was obscured in Eden, and all this entails.

—Maggie Ross

AFTER MY BOOK on Christian mysticism was published in 2010, I was invited to be a guest on a video podcast created by a progressive Christian pastor based in the American Midwest. We had a wonderful conversation about the role of mystical spirituality in the life of faith, especially looking at how mysticism can be a doorway to a felt, intimate experience of God in our lives. Toward the end of our conversation, he asked, "Carl, what is the *one book* you would recommend to anyone who wants to explore Christian mysticism?" He emphasized *one* to be clear he didn't want a list, just the one essential title.

In retrospect, I realize he pitched that particular question as an invitation for me to talk up my own book. But I'm not always the savviest when it comes to marketing (especially self-promotion), so in the moment I just took the question at face value, and I responded to it as honestly as I could. What is the *one* book necessary for the exploration of mystical Christianity? There's really no argument, so I said, "Why, the Bible, of course!"

The host looked nonplussed. Clearly, it wasn't the answer he was expecting. He asked me to elaborate. So I explained that while most Christians today—whether scholars and theologians, ministers and priests, or ordinary laypeople—are not accustomed to thinking of the Bible as a mystical document, when we look at the writings of the great contemplatives, visionaries, and other mystics throughout history, it quickly becomes apparent that they themselves quoted the Bible all the time. It was the heartbeat of their own spiritual growth and development. For them, Scripture was their compass, a manual for living the path of *theosis*, which means a deeply deified and grace-filled mystical life (*deified* is a fancy word for *divine union*).

I've thought about that interview a lot over the years. I have no reason to question the pastor's knowledge of the Bible (or Christian spirituality), but I feel sad that he did not immediately recognize the Bible as a mystical masterpiece. And over the years since then, I've seen again and again that many people, whether they identify as Christian or not, are unaware of the Bible's mystical dimension. I've come to believe that Christians today need to learn a new way of thinking about the Bible and reading it. When we read the Bible like a mystic, we can see that this collection of ancient writings is truly a book calibrated toward not just morality or religious doctrine but also a mind- and heart-expanding transformation of consciousness—the kind of transformation that contemplative prayer or deep silent meditation calls us to. Furthermore, the wisdom of the Bible invites *us* to calibrate *our* lives toward that kind of rich, deep interior transformation that characterized the joy of the great mystics throughout history. In other words, when we read the Bible like a mystic, we not only discover how the mystics experienced God, but we are also invited into that same experience for ourselves.

Remember Karl Rahner's great challenge to the Christians of our time: that in the future, Christians will either be mystics or simply won't exist. With plenty of people giving up on Christianity, it's hard to argue with Rahner, but it raises the question: How do people who truly care about the wisdom teachings of Jesus make the leap from conventional religion to mystical spirituality?

No book by itself can answer this question, this one included. We leap into the mystical life through prayer, silence, and embodied compassion more than through mere reading and study. But I do believe that an important part of reclaiming mystical Christianity in our day will be the vital and necessary work of recognizing the Bible as a mystical masterpiece. This means learning to see the Bible with contemplative eyes. It won't erase all the problems with the challenging passages of the Bible that we looked at in the last chapter, but even those problems look different from a contemplative perspective. Even the most traditional/conservative readers of the Bible know that every verse in the book is not created equal; some simply carry more weight than others. The great mystics throughout history certainly applied this principle to their reading of the Bible, and so should we. Thus, we can dismiss the sexism or homophobia in the Bible as relics of an imperfect past while still celebrating the powerful message of love, hope, faith, justice, forgiveness, and inner growth that forms the Bible's overall message.

When I first learned about Christian mysticism—from reading Evelyn Underhill's 1911 masterpiece, *Mysticism: A Study in the Nature and Development of Spiritual Consciousness*—I realized that I wanted to learn all I could about this ecstatic and luminous approach to spirituality. Underhill's book is based on the writings of the great historical mystics—figures like Julian of Norwich, Meister Eckhart, Catherine of Siena, John of the Cross, Teresa of Ávila, John Ruysbroeck, Catherine of Genoa, and many others. So I began a lifelong project of reading the writings of the great mystics for myself. Of course, it is not necessary to read all (or any) of the great mystics to be contemplative or to engage in practices like meditation and contemplation. But for those who are so inclined, such mystical reading is fascinating and insightful. The mystics are as imperfect as everyone else, so their writings are a glorious mess: passages of shimmering insight are often paired with truly embarrassing views on morality, sin, sexuality and gender, Judaism or other non-Christian religions, and more. Being a mystic does not make one perfect, and unfortunately, those of us who write about our spirituality often leave our imperfections in plain view for the whole world to see. Mystical spirituality calls us into a joyful, embodied union with God, but even the most seasoned or mature mystic can still hold on to ideas or views that are clearly judgmental, dualistic, racist, sexist, homophobic, or simply unloving. We read the mystics not to slavishly follow every single idea or viewpoint they espouse but rather to open our hearts to receive their best and most dazzling wisdom and apply that to our own lives. The rest we criticize fairly and then gently set aside.

If that's what it means to read the writings of the mystics themselves, that's also what it means to read the Bible in a mystical or contemplative manner. We celebrate the wisdom and calmly set aside the rest. To read the Bible like a mystic means reading it to glean as much contemplative inspiration and enlightenment as we might find in the writings of Howard Thurman or Simone Weil or in mystical masterpieces like *The Cloud of Unknowing*.

How do we do this? How do we read the Bible like a mystic? The answer to this question comes from learning to see the Bible in new ways and from new perspectives (at least new for many of us, especially if we come out of a fundamentalist or theologically conservative faith tradition).

A few years before that podcast interview, I attended a conference where Brian McLaren gave a talk on this theme: the things we focus on determine what we miss. To illustrate this point, he had us watch a video featuring a group of basketball players and instructed everyone in the room to pay close attention to how many times the basketballs were being passed back and forth.

There must have been several hundred people in the hotel ballroom where this conference took place. At the end of this short video, McLaren asked us to shout out how many times we counted the basketballs being passed. After everyone shouted out their best guess, he then gave a totally off-the-wall instruction: "Raise your hand if you saw the gorilla."

Only a handful of people did so. He then replayed the video, and sure enough, in the middle of all the basketball players was a man in a monkey suit. Easy to spot—but also easy to miss if you're busy watching something else.

What we focus on determines what we miss. If you are so focused on watching the basketball players, you'll miss the gorilla. The gorilla was hardly invisible, but nearly everyone just filtered it out because our attention was focused elsewhere.

McLaren then applied this principle to how Christians read the Bible. Many people have been taught to read it as an instruction manual for being a good and moral person and for offering a basic story about God's love, humanity's sin, and then redemption through Jesus and sanctification through the Holy Spirit. But this way of reading always seems to point back to individual morality: What does it mean to be a good person? While Christians read the Bible to learn about God, it seems that many believers see this book as primarily a moral instruction manual: how to be a good person in order to be acceptable to God and therefore go to heaven after death.

But the Bible is so much more than just a manual for moral living. McLaren went on to note that many Christians ignore the Bible's teachings on social justice because they are so focused on reading the book only as a manual for individual salvation.

For me, this was an eye-opening presentation, for I immediately saw the contemplative implication here. Because of my own work as a writer (I was working on *The Big Book of Christian Mysticism* at the time), my mind was filled with the writings and ideas of the mystics. Just by sheer osmosis, I was learning to read the Bible in a new way, a contemplative way. But I could see that for most Christians, mysticism in the Bible is like the gorilla in the basketball video. It's hidden in plain sight. We ignore it because we are so busy paying attention to other things.

Which leads us to something Meister Eckhart once said in one of his sermons. Almost offhandedly, this great mystical theologian made a point that I think has profound ramifications for the mystical life. Eckhart said, "The nature of a word is to reveal what is hidden." This is a clue to the mystical meaning of Scripture.

How do words reveal what is hidden? To explore this, let's think about love. When I experience love for someone, it begins as a deep intuition in my heart. It may emerge as a feeling, an insight, a sense of affection or care. When it's romantic love, it can be the heady feelings associated with infatuation or falling in love.

But notice that all of these love experiences are hidden within me. Hopefully I am showing my love with my actions—and yes, I know actions speak louder than words. But there's still a very real sense that until I actually say "I love you" out loud, with my actions or my words—or, at the very least, put it in writing—then the love remains hidden in my heart.

The nature of a word, according to Eckhart, is to reveal what is hidden. Scholars and philosophers will also say that words express power, or set limits, or define what our minds conceive as possible. I have no argument with any of that, but I think Eckhart's wisdom still stands: words reveal to us what has been hidden within the depths of the speaker or writer.

And what is true for the word *love* is true for every word.

If I'm thinking about guacamole, you will have no idea that I am doing so. But then I say, "Let's go get some guac," and thanks to that delicious word, what was hidden in my mind (and appetite) has been revealed.

Pick up a book—any book—and in the reading, you are ushered into the hidden world of the author's mind and heart.

How can we recover the mystical sense of the Bible? How do we learn to see the hidden gorilla of mystical wisdom in a book that we have been conditioned to read in a moralistic way? It may be as simple as reading the mystics (not only of Christianity but also all the world's wisdom traditions) and learning to see things the way they do. It may involve a commitment to *praying* the Bible (reading the Bible as an act of prayer or praying the Liturgy of the Hours, which is largely based on biblical texts) or *praying with* the Bible (by practices like Ignatian prayer or *lectio divina*). But most important of all, I think the first step to reading the Bible like a mystic is simply to bring an open mind and contemplative heart to it. We can pray for spiritual insight, for the Spirit to guide us to sense how the words in the Bible might reveal truth that has been hidden—hidden in the very mind and heart of God.

In his book *A Faith You Can Live With*, Jesuit author John O'Donnell quotes another Jesuit, Philip Rosato, for an insight he made about the articles of faith in the Apostle's Creed: "Each article of faith refers to reality; each touches the believer's personal existence; each has social (communal) consequences; and each contains a dimension of human hope."

What's true for the Creed is also true for the wisdom encoded in the Bible. Every sacred, spiritual, contemplative, and mystical teaching in Scripture has something to say to us on as many as four levels:

- Reality: the way things are
- Hope: the way things could be
- Existence: how this teaching impacts us as individuals
- Consequences: how this teaching impacts us as a collective/community

*   *   *

When Christians call the Bible *the word of God*, this can be seen as a metaphor for Jesus himself but also as a way of understanding Scripture as a wisdom document. Following Eckhart, the word of God reveals (or, at least, has the potential to reveal) what is hidden to us: truths about ourselves, truths about our relationships, truths about present reality, and truths about future possibility. Clearly, not every single word or verse in the Bible carries the same weight—some sections have only historical interest (such as the purity codes or the detailed descriptions of the ark of the covenant), and many of the most difficult passages are weighed down by the limitations of the culture in which they were originally written. So to read the Bible like a mystic, we still need to read it in a careful, informed, discerning way. But when we see it as not just a historical religious document but also as a living text containing spiritual wisdom that invites us into union with God, then the Bible can reveal the greatest "hidden" (mystical) truth of all: that the God who exists is a God who loves us and who seeks union with us, right here and right now.

The Bible itself proclaims that God is love (1 John 4:8, 16). When we read the Bible to reveal the hidden love of God, we read it like a mystic. To do so, we also have to learn to recognize that some passages in the Bible express how humanity often is anything *but* loving and also how sometimes we have mistaken ideas about God (we see God as wrathful, jealous, or vindictive rather than loving). To read the Bible like a mystic, we read it looking to learn more about love—God's love—and also we recognize that sometimes the Bible teaches us about love by showing us what is *not* love. We need to keep reading with a critical mind and a discerning heart, always calibrated toward love.

*   *   *

4

Four Approaches to the Bible

*Individuals ought to portray the ideas of holy Scripture
in a threefold manner upon their own soul. . . . For as
a person consists of body, and soul, and spirit, so in the
same way does Scripture.*

—Origen of Alexandria

I HAVE A friend who used to play the oboe for the Atlanta Symphony Orchestra. He once told me that, as much as he loved music, being a professional changed the way he listened to it. Any time he would hear a symphony, he would naturally pay more attention to the oboe than any other instrument in the orchestra. And it was even worse if it was a recording that he played on—"I keep listening to see if I made any mistakes," he ruefully admitted.

Although I'm no musician, I could understand what he was saying. For a number of years I was a bookstore manager, and to this day, whenever I walk into a bookstore—it could be a big chain operation or a local independent shop—I look at the store with the eye of a bookseller. How is the floor laid out? Is the signage attractive? Is it easy to find the current bestsellers? Sometimes I even check to see if the shelves are lined up well.

Okay, maybe I need to learn to relax and just enjoy browsing (in my defense, there are few pastimes I enjoy more than lazily exploring a good bookstore). But like my friend the musician has learned to listen to music in a new way, I've learned to see a bookstore in a way that probably never crosses the minds of most customers.

So just like not everyone hears a symphony the same way or even experiences a bookstore the same way, not everyone reads the Bible the same way. Depending on our knowledge or expertise, we may pay more attention to certain ideas or themes and even miss other details (like the gorilla in the basketball video). Different people read the Bible in different ways. To read the Bible like a mystic, we need to be aware of some of the many ways to read it.

*   *   *

In the first part of this chapter I want us to consider four broad ways that people of our time read, understand, and interpret the Bible. Any approach you take will ultimately derive from one of these four hermeneutical approaches or some combination of the four. Hermeneutics is a mouthful of a word that means the art and science of interpretation, especially interpretation of a written text. It comes from the Greek word for interpretation, *hermeneuein*, which is derived from the name of the pagan god Hermes, the god of communication, eloquence, and writing. In case you're wondering, hermeneutics is the *theory* of textual interpretation; by contrast, exegesis is the *practice* of interpreting specific texts (like the Bible).

As an academic discipline, hermeneutics reminds us that there is more than one way of interpreting a text (not just the Bible but any text). Later in this chapter we'll look at how one of the great mystics of the early Christian era (third century CE) was aware of this and promoted the idea that you could interpret the Bible in at least three different ways. But I want to begin with a look at how people read the Bible in our time. I believe we can learn a lot just by reflecting on how different approaches to the Bible shed light on the values and ideas we bring to the sacred text before we've even cracked open the cover.

*   *   *

For the purpose of simplicity, I am calling these four ways of reading the Bible the *authoritarian* approach, the *atheist* approach, the *academic* approach, and the *contemplative* approach. None of these labels is perfect, but they work in a general sense to help us recognize four broadly different approaches to biblical interpretation.

*   *   *

I realize that many people will not necessarily identify with one (or any) of these four approaches. Perhaps you identify with more than one (which I think is fine). Some readers might think of themselves as a scholar or an atheist and yet argue that they do not read the Bible exactly the way I describe. Fair enough. Because I'm speaking in broad terms, I'm trying to give a basic outline of the approach that each particular group normally uses. Please see this as a map of how we read the Bible and remember the map is not the territory. This is like primary colors: if you are a printer, you only need four basic colors of ink (cyan, magenta, yellow, and black) to literally print millions of different colors, shades, and hues. Those inks, of course, are similar to the primary colors we learned about in elementary school: blue, red, and yellow. So think of these hermeneutical approaches as the primary colors of Bible reading, realizing that different churches, theologians, scholars, individuals, and yes, mystics, will naturally read the Bible in many different ways.

*   *   *

So let's look at each of these four approaches.

*   *   *

The Authoritarian Approach

Authoritarian (or fundamentalist or "true believer") readers think that the Bible should be literally understood as the inerrant word of God, as if the Spirit were whispering God's thoughts into the minds of the biblical writers. The authoritarian perspective rests on the idea that throughout all of history and all the cultures of the world, God decided that humanity only gets one inerrant book of spiritual teachings, and the Bible is that one book. And for some reason, even when it gets translated into English or any other language, authoritarians still see it as devoid of error (although true believers do love to argue among themselves which translation is the most accurate because that would therefore be the most truly inerrant). Authoritarians have a very hierarchical understanding of God and how the world works; in this way of seeing things, the Bible has absolute and supreme authority because of its status as the unquestionable word of the supreme deity. Our job is not to critique it or try to interpret it in the light of science or other branches of human knowledge but to submissively conform our lives to its demands. Many fundamentalists insist there is no point in interpreting the Bible; you should just look for the "plain meaning" of the text, although the plain meaning is not always so plain. For example, when John the Baptist called Jesus "the Lamb of God" (John 1:29), he was not accusing Christ of being a farm animal. So forgive me for being a little cynical here, but I think when these true believers talk about the "plain meaning" of Scripture, they really mean there's only one acceptable way of reading the Bible: their way.

* * *

The Atheist Approach

Atheist, agnostic, and skeptical readers can be understood as the polar opposite of the fundamentalists and other true believers. The atheists and skeptics believe that empirical science is the only truly reliable source of human knowledge and understanding—for all areas of life, including spirituality (*empirical* means to gain knowledge through observing real-world phenomena rather than relying on religious doctrine or intuition). Such readers not only reject the fundamentalist approach but also go so far as to refuse to consider that there is anything spiritually nourishing in Scripture. They might be willing to accept that some of the stories or poetry might have a limited value as descriptions of human wisdom, but overall they see the Bible as an ancient, outdated, superstitious, and prescientific book that, if anything, is a text to be mocked and derided. Atheists hold that most religious languages and ways of speaking simply cannot pass the test of logical or scientific rigor. I once spent an afternoon on a website called "Why Won't God Heal Amputees?" written by a convinced atheist who uses logic to argue that belief in God must be absurd because God claims to be able to heal anyone, but there has never been a documented case of an amputee getting healed of their missing limb. Clearly, for the person who created this website, it was not enough just to say, "Hmm, religion doesn't make sense to me, so I'll pass." With all the passion and conviction of a fundamentalist preacher, this person set out to prove that Christians are stupid for believing such irrational claims. I'd like to suggest that the atheist approach to the Bible is just as limited as the fundamentalist approach: in many ways, they are mirror images of each other. How sad that so many people never get beyond these two approaches.

*   *   *

The Academic Approach

To read the Bible like an academic scholar, the keys to interpreting the text are history and literary criticism. This means one does not have to be a Christian believer to read the Bible in this way—while certainly many scholars are faithful, practicing Christians, others are agnostics or even atheists or, for that matter, members of other faith traditions. To read the Bible like an academic means to approach it not so much as a text for personal spiritual wisdom but simply to consider it in the light of sociology, psychology, philosophy, archaeology, and other scholarly disciplines. Academics find it interesting to consider what hidden subtexts might be present in any given passage of the Bible, who the intended audience was, how the historical and cultural issues or political concerns of the time impacted what was being said, and so forth. Bible scholars can help us have a more nuanced and meaningful understanding of every verse in the text—including difficult passages like the ones we considered in chapter 2. But even this approach can be limited; the problem with reading the Bible like an academic is that you can get so lost in the abstract meaning of the text that you may no longer be able to read it for personal spiritual meaning—kind of like my friend the oboe player, who got so caught up in the technical issues of musical performance that he could no longer listen to music just for personal enjoyment. To academic scholars, the Bible is primarily a text to be interrogated, often with no end ever in sight.

*   *   *

The Contemplative Approach

To read the Bible like a contemplative means to embrace it as a text filled with mystery and wonder. A contemplative approach rejects both the authoritarian and atheist approaches as too limited or one-dimensional, and while it appreciates the thoughtful knowledge and understanding that the academic approach makes available to us, a contemplative approach remembers that the primary purpose and value of the Bible rests in its spiritual meaning and wisdom—despite its cultural blind spots and limitations. Contemplatives read the Bible not to blindly obey it, or dismissively reject it, or even just to critique it but always primarily as an invitation into the spiritual practice of prayer, meditation, and contemplation. They respect the fact that it was written centuries ago in languages that most of us today do not speak; because of its age, as well as cultural and literary otherness, there is always an element of mystery surrounding the text. A contemplative reading stresses the humility of remembering that there is so much we don't know—not only about the Bible but also about God. But there is still a basic trust that key messages, such as "God is love," "love your neighbors," "be forgiving," and "do not judge," carry universal meaning and therefore can be reliable guideposts for living a spiritually meaningful life today. Contemplatives appreciate the bright light of good scholarship but recognize that the mystery embedded in these ancient Scriptures can never be fully unraveled. For contemplatives, the interplay of the light of reason and the darkness of unknowing is not a problem to be solved but a mystery to be embraced and explored.

*   *   *

Reading the Bible like a mystic means combining the academic knowledge of good Bible scholarship with the spiritual invitation of the contemplative approach, blending these "head" and "heart" approaches to discover the unique way the Bible can speak to each of us individually.

*   *   *

So how do we sort through these different approaches to Bible interpretation? What general principles can we apply to the way we read the sacred text? I'd like to propose three general principles:

1. There is no one right way to read the Bible.
2. Relationships and community matter (how we read the Bible will be shaped by the meaningful relationships and communities in our lives).
3. What we look for will determine what we see (or don't see), especially in terms of love, hope, possibility, and grace.

*   *   *

There Is No One Right Way to Read the Bible

Both the authoritarians and the atheists are going to bristle at this principle because both groups are invested in the idea that their way of reading the text is the only correct way. Everyone who sees the text differently must be mistaken. Both true believers and skeptics read the Bible dualistically, which is to say with an attitude that only one possible interpretation is correct, and all other ways must therefore be mistaken. This approach can feel reassuring, especially if you gather plenty of evidence (and echo chambers) to support your one and only "right" way of interpretation. But the price you pay for believing your way is the only way is a willful disregard of the experiences of others who simply have a different viewpoint and understanding than your own.

The other alternative, which is more challenging psychologically but healthier on an ethical and communal level, is to recognize that good people sometimes see the world differently and therefore will disagree—and even disagree radically. Once we accept this, we can begin to move from debate (where we try to prove who's right and who's wrong) to dialogue (where we humbly attempt to understand each other and learn from one another). This is difficult work, but it is necessary work. And it leads to the second principle: that we need each other to effectively read the Bible (or any great book of spiritual wisdom).

*   *   *

Community and Relationships Matter

Imagine you have a friend whom you know dearly; you know from experience that this person is kind and loving. You've known them for years, and while they are not perfect (no one is), they are the type of person who tries to always do their best and learn from their mistakes.

Then one day someone else writes something about this friend that says that far from being kind and loving, they are filled with rage and anger. You know that the person who wrote this is mistaken, and you know it because you know your friend so well. But unfortunately, the article has been published widely, and other people who don't know your friend very well read it without understanding how misinformed (or malicious) the author is.

All these people begin to form opinions about your friend based just on this one article. Then they start talking among themselves about how angry and wrathful your friend is. Maybe one or two of them had an experience with your friend on one of their bad days, and so they add fuel to the fire, and soon everyone is convinced that your friend is simply a mean, rotten, angry, and vicious person who should be shunned.

You realize that you cannot prevent that misunderstanding from spreading, but you also have to be clear that your experience does not align with what has been written. You have to be true to your experience, which means you interpret what was written in a radically different way from all those people who don't know your friend. Perhaps you (and your community, which includes other people who appreciate your friend's loving nature) can write new articles that show your friend's loving qualities, and if enough of these articles get circulated, perhaps the damage of the misinformed/malicious article can be lessened. In other words, it takes the entire community and the relationships that hold the community together to get to the truth of what's going on.

Relying on each other to understand human nature—or an ancient spiritual text like the Bible—is messy. We all have different perspectives and values and naturally see or emphasize different things in how we navigate our lives. A community will never find the "one, true" meaning of the Bible or any other text. For mystics, accustomed to seeking the wonder and the mystery in Scripture, this is not a problem and actually can be seen as a blessing. Consider these words of wisdom from a Bible scholar, Sandra Schneiders: "Consequently, there is no such thing as *the* one correct interpretation of a text. Texts are susceptible of endless new interpretations as different interpreters, with different questions and different backgrounds, interrogate the text about its subject matter. There is also no one correct method or constellation of methods for interpreting a text." Learning to trust the wisdom and insight of others who read the Bible from a different perspective than your own takes dedication and hard work, and it forces us to see not only the Bible but also God and the world from a larger perspective. But when we do this, our appreciation of the wisdom in the Bible grows deeper.

* * *

What We Look for Determines What We See (or Miss)

Brian McLaren's talk helps to shed light on the four approaches to the Bible that I've described. Fundamentalists look for evidence of God as an authoritarian father figure, while atheists (if they bother reading the Bible at all) look for evidence that it is backward and superstitious. Scholars read it looking for academic problems to solve, while contemplatives read it looking for a deeper encounter with the mystery of God.

Reading the Bible like a mystic means learning to notice, and pay attention to, the mystical wisdom that shows up in the text. Think of it this way: when you buy a new car, sometimes you'll be amazed at how many times you notice cars just like yours on the road. They've always been there; you just haven't been paying attention until now. The Bible works the same way. If you read it looking for evidence of God's love, hope, possibility, and grace, that will shape how you read the Bible. Conversely, if you read it looking for judgment, condemnation, conditional love, and systems of reward and punishment, that's what you'll see instead. Reading the Bible like a mystic means reading it with eyes calibrated to love.

Origen of Alexandria's Three Ways of Reading the Bible

*   *   *

Attempts to limit the Bible to just one "plain" meaning do a disservice to the rich and nuanced content of Scripture. Fortunately, the mystics agree with me. Even back in the third century, Christian mystics like Origen of Alexandria (185–ca. 253 CE) understood that you can't just limit the Bible to one way of interpretation.

*   *   *

In addition to being an early mystic, Origen was also a renowned (and controversial) theologian and Bible scholar. He suggested that the Bible needs to be read on three levels: the literal, the moral, and the mystical. With apologies to those who insist on reading and interpreting the Bible simplistically, Christian mystics have known for well over 1,750 years that any passage of Scripture can be interpreted in at least three different ways. If you want to have an honest encounter with God, then you need to begin with an honest recognition that the Bible can always be read and understood in multiple ways.

* * *

It's important to understand the distinctions among these three approaches to the Scriptures. It's also important *not* to jump to conclusions concerning what *literal* and *moral* (or, for that matter, *mystical*) mean. In affirming the literal meaning, Origen is *not* saying that we should read the Bible in a fundamentalist way. He is simply acknowledging that sometimes it is helpful to understand the Bible at face value. Nor is he suggesting that a moral reading of Scripture is just about placing limits on our behavior or, worse yet, trying to identify who is at risk of being rejected by God. Rather, the moral reading challenges all of us to remember that the Bible offers us a transformed way of seeing things (including ethical situations)—learning to see all things through the vantage point of divine love. Here is one way to approach Origen's different ways of reading the Bible:

- The literal reading of the Bible means seeking to understand it on a purely natural level. This is not the fundamentalist approach but is actually more like the scholarly or academic reading of the text. The literal reading is an attempt to understand what the original writer(s) meant, the social and cultural background of what they were saying, and the philosophical and theological foundation (and implications) of their words. This approach to reading Scripture takes into consideration a nuanced understanding of the original languages, the literary genre the writer is employing, and the intended audience and its needs and concerns. The literal reading is just as important as the moral and mystical readings, which are more subjective and spiritual in their approach to the text. The literal/scholarly reading keeps faith grounded and centered.

- The moral reading of the Bible brings the meaning and purpose of the text into the life of the individual reader. Here the focus is less on an objective, scholarly understanding of the text in favor of a more subjective, inspirational understanding. What does this passage say *to me*? How does it offer me a sense of meaning and purpose? How does it help me shape the choices and commitments of my life? How can it help me form my character? How does it help me be a better person? If Origen's literal reading is akin to the scholarly approach to the Bible, then his moral reading corresponds to what I'm calling the contemplative approach. The common contemplative practice of *lectio divina* is an exercise in this way of reading the Bible—although, as we shall see, *lectio divina* also invites us into the mystical reading as well.

- The mystical reading of the Bible invites readers to consider hidden, obscure, or symbolic ways of finding meaning in the text—especially in the light of God's desire for loving intimacy with us. Just as the moral reading of the text offers the reader a subjective, inspirational way of understanding the Scriptures, the mystical reading invites us into an *intersubjective* and *transfigurative* approach to the text. How does this text reveal God's love? How does it testify to the hidden realities that we, as Christians, accept as a matter of faith: that God loves us, that God brings us unconditional healing, that God desires intimacy with us, that God call us to union with God—and all this held together in the person of Christ, the sacrament of God-with-us. So a mystical reading of Scripture looks for hidden resonances of meaning but always centered on the experience of God as both mystery and divine love.

*   *   *

To summarize, the literal reading looks for what is objectively factual about the text, what can be understood in the light of the best historical and critical scholarship; the moral reading looks for how the text can be inspirational and personally meaningful to the reader; and the mystical reading looks for hidden ways in which the text can support God's desire for union with us, both individually and collectively. The literal meaning is focused on the text itself, the moral reading is focused on the reader and their response to the text, and the mystical reading is focused on God and God's loving action.

*   *   *

An Example of the Three Ways of Reading Scripture

As an example of these three complementary approaches to Scripture, let's look at Exodus 3:1–5, one of the most famous passages in the Bible:

> *Moses was keeping the flock of his father-in-law*
> *Jethro, the priest of Midian; he led his flock beyond*
> *the wilderness, and came to Horeb, the mountain of*
> *God. There the angel of the Lord appeared to him in*
> *a flame of fire out of a bush; he looked, and the bush*
> *was blazing, yet it was not consumed. Then Moses*
> *said, "I must turn aside and look at this great sight,*

and see why the bush is not burned up." When the
Lord saw that he had turned aside to see, God called
to him out of the bush, "Moses, Moses!" And he said,
"Here I am." Then he said, "Come no closer! Remove
the sandals from your feet, for the place on which you
are standing is holy ground."

The literal reading asks questions like: What is going on here? Did the bush really burn, or is this a folktale? Could this be a description of a dream? Is it a legend designed to enhance Moses's reputation as someone who spoke with God? Perhaps there was an optical illusion or even an actual slow-burning fire that inspired Moses to experience an imaginal encounter with God. Of course, none of these speculative theories can ever be conclusively proven, so many scholars will simply accept that this story represents a key, if mysterious, event in the life of the person who is seen as a liberator of the Hebrew people.

The moral meaning takes a more subjective approach. It asks, "What would I do if *I* encountered the burning bush?" It speculates that this story shows that anyone—not just heroes like Moses—might receive a theophany, or encounter with God. Maybe such a theophany might have a supernatural quality, like seeing a burning bush, but it might just as well have a more interior, imaginal (but entirely down-to-earth) quality—and either way, it can transform the person who receives this encounter in radical ways. For example, Mother

Teresa of Calcutta never saw a burning bush (at least to my knowledge), but she did experience an *internal* sense of being called by God—which led to her living a life of service and healing that in its own way is just as dramatic as the story of Moses. So the moral meaning invites us to reflect on this idea that God could speak to *us* too—and if/when God does, will we be ready? Will we be able to listen? Will we be free to truly and fully respond?

Finally, the mystical reading of the text seeks to find hidden meanings, particularly from a divine perspective. It might begin by drawing a connection between the miracle of the burning bush and Jesus proclaiming, "I am the light of the world." God not only wants to speak with us, but God also wants to bring light into our lives: the light of truth, of clarity, of healing, of liberation. God brought light into Moses's life, and Moses was changed forever—and that change has echoed down through the ages. God desires all of us to be the same agents for freedom and liberation that Moses was, even if for most of us it will play out in far less dramatic ways. There's even another hidden layer, for not only did Christ say, "*I* am the light of the world," but he also proclaimed, "*You* are the light of the world" (John 8:12; Matthew 5:14). God is calling Moses to *be* light by bringing a message of freedom and liberation to his people. God makes similar calls to all of us. And by calling us to *be* light—the same light that Christ manifests—God is also calling us to be *one with Christ*, which is to say, *one with God*.

This is just one example of how a passage can be read in three different ways: from the perspective of the scholar/historian, from the perspective of an individual contemplative seeker, and then finally from the perspective of God, which is always ultimately a mystery to us, but through love and imagination we might be able to catch a glimpse of the divine perspective. Each of these perspectives is valuable in its own way, although, naturally, the literal reading involves a kind of empirical objectivity that is different from the spiritual subjectivity of the moral and mystical readings. This doesn't mean the moral and mystical readings are "anything goes." Each reading needs to be done in the light of the other approaches, and our individual/subjective readings also need to be discerned in the light of the wisdom of tradition. Equally important is the role of community: we help each other discern the meaning of the sacred text, whether historical, personal, or divine.

* * *

5

Miracles, Myth, and Imagination

Imagination is your interior sense . . . imagination is not fantasy, imagination is creative.

—Thomas Merton

* * *

ONE OF THE reasons that many people have a hard time taking the Bible seriously—and opt to read it from the cynical perspective of atheists and other skeptics—is because of the many stories found within its pages that are filled with magical or supernatural elements. If you find the miracles and wonders in biblical stories to be just too much to swallow, then this chapter is for you. On the other hand, if the Bible's larger-than-life stories don't particularly bother you (or even if you like them), this chapter is meant to help all of us look at how we can reconcile an empirical or scientific way of thinking with the tales of the miraculous found in Scripture.

* * *

What about the Miracles?

*   *   *

Many people who are exposed to the Bible's stories, even as children, sooner or later might find themselves asking questions like these:

- Did a talking snake really speak to the first human woman and convince her to eat a forbidden food?
- Did a flood really wipe out all of life on the planet except for the inhabitants of one gigantic boat?
- Did Moses really see a bush burn without being consumed?
- Did the walls of Jericho collapse merely at the sound of a trumpet blast?
- Did Daniel survive a night in a den of lions?
- Did Jesus walk on water?
- Did he feed thousands of people with merely a few loaves and fishes?
- Did he raise Lazarus from the dead?
- And for that matter, was he himself bodily resurrected, able to walk through walls and appear and disappear at will?
- Did he ascend bodily into heaven after promising his followers he would return at the end of time?

These questions relate to just a few of the many wonderous stories found in the Bible, both the Old and New

Testaments, that many people might find a bit hard to swallow.

*   *   *

Biblical fundamentalists and other true believers would respond to such questions like this: "Of course those things really happened; the Bible is the word of God, and therefore it must be true." Meanwhile, the atheist reader might reply, "Hogwash! Clearly these stories are superstitious fables, holdovers from a primitive, prescientific culture incapable of understanding how the universe really worked." Academic scholars might join in by saying, "Actually these stories are folktales, ancient myths designed to explain mysterious aspects of human life or to embellish the devotion that the biblical writers felt for people like Moses or Jesus." Contemplative readers might just say, "Maybe it's a mistake to worry about whether these stories are historically true; their purpose is to help us to discover *spiritual* meaning in our lives today."

*   *   *

I'll make a confession. Although I have deep respect for science and empirical ways of thinking, I believe in miracles. I believe life itself is a miracle, and I believe love is a miracle. Therefore, I can't just summarily reject the Bible's extraordinary stories just because they seem incredible by modern standards. But since I do have such respect for science and scholarship, I also can't just blindly insist that such stories must be factually true just because the Bible says so. When I read the stories of miracles in the Bible, if you ask me if I believe they really (historically) happened, the most honest answer I can give you is "I don't know."

*   *   *

Thousands of years after the fact, we simply cannot prove one way or the other whether any of the miracles in the Bible ever took place in an objective, factual, "it really happened" kind of way. Those who are scientifically minded will scoff and dismiss all of these stories as, at best, quaint legends that are holdovers from a less sophisticated time. On the other hand, biblical fundamentalists and other true-believer Christians will not only loudly proclaim that they accept these stories; they will also tell you that the ability to believe is itself a gift from God—the gift of faith—and if you don't have that gift, well, too bad for you.

*   *   *

Those lines seem pretty hard-drawn. Either you're a committed believer or a convinced skeptic. A person of faith or an agnostic (or atheist). A sheep or a goat.

*   *   *

But perhaps there is another, more helpful way of thinking about the stories in the Bible that charts a middle course between "these things really happened" and "they're just a bunch of fairy tales." This involves what we can call the *spiritual imagination.* This is a key to the contemplative approach to the Bible—and also the mystical approach.

*   *   *

The imagination is our capacity to create experiences within the human mind. Such experiences can be utterly fictitious—for example, I like to imagine what it would be like to live five hundred years in the future—or they can be rough drafts of a possible life that is actually within our grasp, like imagining embarking on a trip around the world next year. Just because you've imagined something doesn't guarantee it will happen in real life—I am serenely confident that I will die many years before 2525 rolls around. On the other hand, some of our imaginings just might manifest as "real" experiences—my round-the-world vacation hasn't happened yet, but it remains firmly on my bucket list.

The imagination can take us anywhere, not just into the future. We can imagine the past, we can imagine what life might be like for people in another part of the world, and we can even imagine the experiences of animals, plants, angels, and aliens. The only limits to the imagination are the limits we place on it ourselves.

*   *   *

When we talk about the *spiritual* imagination, we're taking it even a step further. This is a type of imagination that takes us to a realm of inner experiences that simply can never be proven true or false. What would it be like to experience God at work in your own heart? What is God's personality like? If you could have a chat with God, what would the two of you talk about?

* * *

Now take this principle of the spiritual imagination and see how it can shed light on the questions I listed above. Did a supreme being create the world in a mere six earthly days? Somebody, somewhere, imagined that this could be true and wrote it down. Enough other people resonated with that imagination that the story has been kept alive now for millennia. Yes, some people think it's nonsense, and others got so caught up in it that they assumed it must be as true as any measurable scientific fact. But these interpretations of the story both miss the point. It's not meant to be science, and it's not meant to be a lie. It's meant to be an *imaginal inspiration.*

* * *

So all the miraculous and supernatural stories that are recounted in the Bible—from the creation stories in Genesis to the descent of the New Jerusalem in the closing chapters of Revelation—are all real experiences but "real" in terms of being experiences of the spiritual imagination. Some of them may, in fact, be partially or entirely based on historical events, even if the story as it ends up in the Bible has been embellished and supersized. There are Bible scholars who devote their lives and careers to trying to figure out which events described in the Bible are historical and which ones aren't. It's an interesting academic exercise, although no one can ever definitely prove once and for all where the line separating history from myth falls—and I would argue that getting caught up in trying to chart that line may be academically intriguing, but from a mystical perspective, such theoretical speculation is actually an exercise in missing the point—because the point behind the spiritual imagination is not to reveal solid historical or scientific facts but rather to inspire us to imagine, experience, and encounter truth, goodness, and beauty as they can be found deep within. Truth, goodness, and beauty are universal qualities that give life meaning, purpose, and joy but that can never be reduced to a scientific formulation or empirical evidence. That's because truth, goodness, and beauty are natural elements of the spiritual imagination: they cannot be measured or observed with a scientific instrument, for they exist primarily in our hearts and minds, and they exist to give us meaning and value in our lives.

* * *

To read the Bible like a mystic means to read it through the visionary lens of our own spiritual imagination. For those of us who are accustomed to reading in a more scientific or empirical way—looking for facts and just the facts—it may be an adjustment to learn to read in an openhearted, imaginative way. Did Jesus walk on water? I don't know.

But I know that in someone's spiritual imagination he did. And I know that in *my* spiritual imagination it only makes sense that someone widely revered as the ultimate human embodiment (incarnation) of God would be able to list walking on water on his résumé. It really doesn't change my life very much to think about Jesus walking on water or to assume that he couldn't walk on water. But when I read Jesus telling people to be merciful and forgiving, and to be kind even to our enemies, and to refrain from being judgmental, arrogant, and hostile to others—when I apply those words of wisdom to my life, they *do* make a difference. And if imagining Jesus as someone who can walk on water and raise people from the dead makes it easier for me to take his wisdom teachings seriously, then I am all for the spiritual imagination—because at the end of the day, what matters most to any human being, when it comes to living a spiritual life (or not), is our *own* imagination. The people who wrote the Bible had powerful and richly detailed spiritual imaginations, and their stories and myths have caught the imagination of generations of biblical scholars, commentators, teachers, and preachers, let alone the many ordinary people like you and me who have tried to live our lives according to the wisdom that the Bible offers us. But those many generations of imaginative writers, thinkers, and teachers would not mean a thing if my own imagination wasn't in some way inspired by theirs.

*   *   *

This, at root, is the difference between believers and nonbelievers. Believers have imaginations that say yes to the great lineage of spiritual wisdom and visionary insight that has been handed down to us, generation after generation. Nonbelievers say, "Uh, no thank you." Fundamentalists, like atheists, do not understand that the imagination can convey spiritual truth even if it is not "historically true." But where atheists just dismiss the myths that inspire the spiritual imagination as hogwash, fundamentalists insist that these myths aren't myths at all but are meant to be read as real events that happened in space and time. Meanwhile, those whose faith leans more toward the contemplative and mystical understanding can appreciate the mythic imagination without confusing inner mythic truth with the scientific world of observable facts.

*   *   *

Tragically, many people reject the imaginative wisdom of the Bible (and other spiritual traditions) because it has been presented to them as a matter of historical fact and that they have only two choices: believe it as objective fact or reject it out of hand. Clearly, many intelligent, reasonable people find it less intellectually dishonest to simply reject the mythology of the Bible than to attempt to assent to something that they conscientiously believe could not be historically accurate. This is the church's fault: too many Christians have become so dogmatically rigid in our thinking that we expect everyone else to see things the way we do, and then we get annoyed when they are true to their own conscience and see things differently. Rather than investigating that with an open mind, we get entrenched in seeing the world dualistically: some people have faith, and others don't; by this way of thinking, some people are sheep, and some are goats. And much suffering has ensued because of that black/white thinking.

*   *   *

To read the Bible like a mystic, think of the miracles and supernatural stories as masterpieces of the spiritual imagination. If you want to imagine that they are also historically factual, that is your prerogative. Many intelligent and well-educated people of faith choose to believe that many (if not all) of the miracle stories are based on facts. But you don't have to accept such stories as factual in order to find spiritual meaning within them—and many of us find that the true meaning and message of these stories simply do not require them to be historical. Maybe Jesus never bodily rose from the tomb—but when I imagine that he did, it gives me a sense of hope and possibility. If I lose my job or I experience a serious illness, I can trust that after these difficult losses, there's hope for a brighter tomorrow. I can also project that hope and trust into my imagination of what happens after my physical death. None of us knows what awaits us after death. But the spiritual imagination of many people from every generation and the world over has encouraged us to trust and believe that death is not the end. This gives millions of people hope, and such hope is both beautiful and inspiring. No one knows what ultimately happens after we die, and from that place of I-don't-know, believing in life after death is just as plausible as believing death is the end. So my imagination allows me to entertain the possibility that gives me a sense of hope.

*   *   *

The next time you read the Bible and you encounter a story that seems incredible, don't ask, "Is this true?" Instead ask, "What could this mean?" This question invites *your* imagination to engage with the possible message or messages embedded in that story. Instead of worrying about what did (or did not) empirically happen thousands of years ago, consider what kind of a difference the spiritual message of the story could make in your life today. I don't know if God created the world in six days, but it's meaningful for me to imagine that the universe was created out of love. I don't know if a snake tempted Eve, but it's meaningful for me to imagine that our actions sometimes have unintended consequences. I don't know if Jesus fed five thousand people with five loaves and two fishes, but I imagine that believing in miracles can inspire ordinary people to do some pretty amazing things. And I don't know if Jesus died for my sins, but I find that my imagination is filled with hope by the message that God would love me enough to die for me— and maybe, therefore, I can aspire to embody love like that in my life as well.

*   *   *

Spirituality, ultimately, is about so much more than just knowing some facts and having opinions about history. It's about living a life transformed by love and mercy, care and compassion, faithfulness and forgiveness. And these qualities may shape how we relate to whatever we imagine God to be, but they really make a difference in terms of how we relate to one another. If the miracle stories can inspire the spiritual imagination of people like you and me to be more loving, kinder, and more compassionate, then I say bring them on.

6

Guidance from the Mystics

If you would grasp Christ, you will do so sooner by following him than by reading of him. . . . Believe me as one who has experience, you will find much more among the woods than ever you will among books. Woods and stones will teach you what you can never hear from any master.

—Bernard of Clairvaux

*   *   *

IF ANYONE CAN teach us how to read the Bible like a mystic, it's the mystics themselves. In chapter 4, we saw how one of the earliest of Western mystics, Origen of Alexandria, taught us a multilevel approach to reading Scripture. Now I want to briefly introduce you to some of the wisdom from other leading mystics in the Western world.

*   *   *

The writings of the mystics reveal that they are a varied and diverse bunch. Someone (I'm not sure who said it first) said, "Mystics are not a special kind of human being; rather, each human being is a special kind of mystic." Some mystics are saints; others have been accused of heresy. Some are great poets, theologians, and philosophers; others are completely down-to-earth and ordinary. Some are nuns and monks; others lead secular lives. And of course, mystics come from every century, every nation and continent, representing every age, gender, ethnicity, and social status. There's no "one-size-fits-all" in the mystical life—and so there is no one standard way that mystics read the Bible (or do practically anything else).

* * *

This, friends, is good news. To read the Bible like the mystics, we need to learn to read it authentically and consistently with our own unique and individual perspective, our own understanding of God, and faith, and what it means to be responsive to the Spirit in our lives. Yes, you won't do it exactly the same as I will, and neither one of us will read Scripture the way Hildegard of Bingen, Howard Thurman, or Francis of Assisi did—thank heaven.

* * *

I think anyone interested in how the mystics read Scripture would benefit from seeing some of the different ways that mystics down the centuries have approached the Bible—not because we have to do it exactly the way they did but because we can learn a thing or two from most of the mystics, and their wisdom, insight, and example can help us as we seek to make Bible reading uniquely our own.

*   *   *

I led with Origen of Alexander because his three-methods approach gives us a model for being both honest and faith-filled as we encounter the wisdom and also the challenges in Scripture. Here is a quick survey of how other mystics have read the Bible, beginning with one of the mystics in the New Testament and coming all the way up to the twentieth century.

*   *   *

Read the Bible like Saint Paul

The apostle Paul is widely regarded as a mystic, thanks to the extraordinary encounters he had with Christ and God as recorded in the Acts of the Apostles (his conversion on the Road to Damascus) and 2 Corinthians 12 (his account of being caught up "to the third heaven"). But Paul also provides a wonderful example, in the Bible itself, of how it is appropriate to interpret—and reinterpret—Scripture. In Galatians 4:22–31, Paul recounts a story found in the book of Genesis— the story of Abraham's two children from two different mothers (Genesis 16 and 21)—and interprets it using another passage, this time from the prophet Isaiah (54:1), to make a point about his understanding of the relationship between legalism and grace in the spiritual life. Most scholars feel that Paul's interpretation is not a traditional understanding, certainly from the perspective of Jewish commentators. It's not my purpose here to weigh the merits of Paul's interpretation but simply to point out that interpreting the Bible to find a spiritual meaning that may be different from the literal meaning goes all the way back to the apostles. Using Origen's model, Paul gives us an example of reading Genesis 16 and 21 from Origen's moral perspective—in other words, reading the text to find personal meaning and personal spiritual insight.

*   *   *

Read the Bible like Saint Benedict or Guigo II

If Paul demonstrated how to read the Bible for finding spiritual meanings, two Western monks—Benedict of Nursia (sixth century) and Guigo II (twelfth century)—emphasized this contemplative approach as a way to truly discover mystical wisdom in Scripture. Benedict simply endorses that reading the Bible is so important that every monk should do it (remember, he was writing at a time when books were rare and valuable; what he endorsed for monks and nuns would apply to everyone today), but a lesser-known monk, Guigo II, wrote an essay called "The Ladder of Monks," which provides a step-by-step guide to prayer, as well as a meditative and contemplative approach to reading the Bible. Guigo's method is known as *lectio divina* (from the Latin, meaning *sacred reading*), and it is still commonly taught to monks and other spiritual seekers to this day. Benedict and Guigo seem to be telling us that in order to read the Bible like a mystic, we ought to *pray* the words of the Bible and use them as a springboard for meditation and inner reflection.

* * *

Read the Bible like Pseudo-Dionysius

One of the most mysterious mystical teachers in the history of Christianity is Pseudo-Dionysius, who lived around the year 500. We don't know this mystic's real name; he ascribed his writings to a very minor figure in the New Testament, Dionysius the Areopagite (who is only mentioned one time in the entire Bible). To our modern sensibilities, it looks like Pseudo-Dionysius was trying to pretend to be someone he wasn't, which strikes us as dishonest, but most scholars think he was actually motivated by humility, not wanting to use his real name and choosing a super-obscure person in the Bible to hide his identity behind (if he really was trying to fool his readers into thinking his writing was important, he would have claimed his words belonged to a major biblical figure like Paul or Peter). It probably never occurred to Pseudo-Dionysius that his writings would be passed down from generation to generation, and eventually he became renowned as a major mystic and important theological writer.

Pseudo-Dionysius insisted that we can never fully express with human words what God *is*, but we can only acknowledge how our language limits us from knowing the fullness of God; therefore, it is safer for us to use our human language and logic to try to describe what God is *not*. In the words of the 1909 Catholic Encyclopedia, Pseudo-Dionysius held "that the names of God are to be learned from Scripture only, and that they afford us but an imperfect knowledge of God." This powerful perspective maintained that even the Bible gives us only an "imperfect" knowledge of God. So to read the Bible like Pseudo-Dionysius we must remember that finite human language cannot encompass the limitless infinity of the creator of the universe—not even in the book reputed to be God's word. Therefore we need to read the Bible with humility, a humility that recognizes God is always bigger than our names for God, our images of God, and our thoughts and concepts about God.

Incidentally, Pseudo-Dionysius influenced many great mystics who came after him, including the anonymous author of *The Cloud of Unknowing*, the great Spanish mystic Saint John of the Cross, and even mystics in the modern era, like Evelyn Underhill or Hans Urs von Balthasar.

* * *

Read the Bible like Saint Augustine

I've pointed out how authoritarian and fundamentalist "true believers" are uncomfortable with the idea that passages in the Bible can be legitimately interpreted in multiple ways. This

idea is not just the product of postmodern relativism—it goes
all the way back to the fourth century and the words of Saint
Augustine, widely regarded as one of the most influential
of early-church theologians (and who, incidentally, was also
a mystic). Augustine saw the Bible as a limitless treasury of
meaning—like Saint Teresa of Ávila, who said that every word
contained a thousand mysteries. In other words, there is no
end to the ways the Bible can be read or understood. This is
so important that I want to let Augustine speak to this in his
own voice.

> So when one person has said "Moses thought what I
> say," and another "No, what I say," I think it more
> religious in spirit to say "Why not rather say both, if
> both are true?" And if anyone sees a third or fourth
> and a further truth in these words, why not believe
> that Moses discerned all these things? For through
> him the one God has tempered the sacred books
> to the interpretations of many, who could come to
> see a diversity of truths. Certainly, to make a bold
> declaration from my heart, if I myself were to be
> writing something at this supreme level of authority I
> would choose to write so that my words would sound
> out with whatever diverse truth in these matters
> each reader was able to grasp, rather than to give a
> quite explicit statement of a single true view of this
> question in such a way as to exclude other views.

How many times do people argue over what this or that verse in the Bible could mean? When we read the Bible like Augustine, we don't have to take an "anything goes" approach, but we can recognize that many passages in the Bible might have multiple ways to be interpreted. No one person (or church) has a lock on the truth.

* * *

Read the Bible like Saint Hildegard of Bingen

Hildegard of Bingen was a renowned nun who lived in the twelfth century; she was an herbalist, a musician (most of her music still gets recorded today), and, of course, a great mystic. She described herself as a "feather on the breath of God." Her writings are deeply visionary and quite distinctive in how she understands God and the work of the Spirit in the world. Bernard McGinn points out that Hildegard "tells how in 1141 she received 'a fiery light of exceeding brilliance' from heaven that penetrated her whole brain and heart and gave her immediate knowledge of the meaning of the Bible." I understand that most of us will likely never experience "fiery light" that will give us that kind of immediate knowledge, but Hildegard does suggest that we can trust our intuition to guide us when we read the Bible. Some Christians won't like this idea because there is within the church a long tradition of teaching people *not* to trust their intuition. We cannot assume our intuition is infallible, so we need to discern the guidance of our intuition through the shared wisdom of others (in other words, we learn how to interpret the Bible through the wisdom of our communities). Still, even with that caveat in mind, Hildegard's experience is empowering: sometimes the best way to know what the Bible is saying, especially to us personally, is to inquire within.

*   *   *

Read the Bible like Julian of Norwich

Another great woman mystic of the Middle Ages, Julian lived in the fourteenth and early fifteenth centuries and wrote the first book by a woman in the English language, her *Revelations of Divine Love*. Like Hildegard of Bingen, Julian represents someone who learned to trust her own inner guidance when it came to reading the Bible. In trusting her own inner guidance, she was able to express some truly visionary insights into the Bible (and faith in general) that continue to be cutting-edge, even today. Julian shows us how her mystical approach to the Bible led her inner intuition and guidance to engage in a kind of holy conversation with Scripture.

*   *   *

Julian's visions are rich expressions of her inner experience of God, Christ, and the Spirit. She does not directly talk about reading or commenting on the Bible, which makes sense given that her experience of the Bible was probably limited to hearing it read publicly when she went to church. But at least one time, she makes a bold statement that not only offers a new way of thinking about God but also points to a new way of reading the Bible.

*   *   *

Julian remarks that her visions gave her a new perspective on an idea about God—an idea that probably was quite common in her fourteenth century experience of Christianity: the notion of "the wrath of God." Julian writes, "I saw no kind of wrath in God, neither for a short time nor for long. (For truly, as I see it, if God were to be angry even a hint, we would never have life nor place nor being.) As truly as we have our being from the endless Power of God and from the endless Wisdom, and from the endless Goodness, just as truly we have our protection in the endless Power of God, in the endless Wisdom, and in the endless Goodness."

Elsewhere in her writing, Julian notes, "I saw no wrath except on humanity's part, and that God forgives in us. For wrath is nothing else but a rebellion from and an opposition to peace and to love, and either it comes from the failure of power or from the failure of wisdom, or from the failure of goodness (which failure is not in God but it is on our part)."

It's a compelling argument. There's no such thing as wrath in God! Furthermore, when human beings have *thought*

we saw wrath in God, Julian is basically saying that we are projecting our own human anger on to God, for God is perfect
power, wisdom, and goodness, and anger stems from a "failure" of power, wisdom, or goodness in human hearts.

There's only one problem with what Julian is saying, and
that is how full the Bible is of images of God that seem quite
wrathful indeed. Both in the Old and New Testaments, concepts like "the wrath of God" appear again and again. Is Julian
just mistaken here? After all, as a woman in the Middle Ages,
she probably never studied the Bible, certainly not like priests
or scholars would have.

Remember Saint Augustine and his contention that there
is more than one way to interpret many passages of the Bible.
What if the Bible's many different voices and stories and perspectives on God represent a kind of documented history of
how our spiritual ancestors (the ancient Jews and the earliest
Christians) actually grew and evolved in their understanding
of God? Certainly their perspectives changed over time (this is
why some passages seem to contradict other passages).

Perhaps the Bible is a book that shows us that our understanding of God, and truth, and spirituality grew and evolved
over the centuries in which the Bible was written—and continues *to evolve to this day.*

So rather than getting caught up on what is absolutely
the "one correct way" of reading the Bible, we can approach
the Bible as a work in progress—as the word of God that is
still being spoken. Like any good story, we can expect character

development—only in the Bible, it's not so much that God's character is developing but rather that the *human understanding of God is growing and evolving.* Some images of God in the Bible are, obviously enough, going to be more helpful than others—some might be more obsolete, more culturally conditioned, more shaped by outdated ideas where God is seen as terrifying, angry, patriarchal, wrathful—compared to other images found within the Bible that stress God as loving, merciful, kind, and radically forgiving.

Like Hildegard of Bingen, Julian was a mystic who trusted her own inner guidance. She was a devout Christian, so naturally she knew that the Bible has language in it that claims God is filled with wrath. But when, during her visionary experience, she had a powerful sense of God as loving and compassionate, she trusted her intuition even though it appeared to disagree with the teachings she got from the Bible.

Julian very simply states, "I saw no wrath in God," followed by "I saw no wrath except on man's part." I think we need to hold both statements together to understand what Julian is saying. Clearly, Julian is engaging in her own exegesis; in other words, *Julian is interpreting the Bible based on her own visionary experience of God.* She is challenging us to rethink what the very concept of "the wrath of God" as found in the Bible means.

There's plenty of language in the Bible about God's wrath. But there's also plenty of language in the Bible stressing God's love, mercy, compassion, and forgiveness. Are we to assume that God is moody—angry some of the time but understanding and forgiving the rest of the time? That sure sounds like projecting a human quality (the changeable nature of our emotions) on to God.

Julian offers a different interpretation. She boldly suggests that "the wrath of God" is essentially a *mirror of human wrath*— we human beings project our anger onto God, and then when we imagine what God's personality must be like, our image of God functions like a mirror, causing us to see our own anger in what appears to be God's wrath. Human beings—including biblical writers—are prone to assuming that God is basically a mirror image of ourselves. Since human beings get angry and wrathful, God must too, and biblical writers inserted this projection into their way of speaking about God. But Julian, based on the authority of her mystical experience of God, isn't having it. She calls us to a new way of seeing God.

Julian reasonably argues, "If God were to be angry even a hint, we would never have life nor place nor being." In other words, the wrath of God would simply annihilate all existence. We are held in existence by God's creativity, God's love, and God's sustenance. Her point is: *if God really got angry, we would be completely and utterly annihilated by the terrible force of that wrath.*

Therefore, God may judge us, God may hold us accountable for our sins, and God may expect us to take responsibility for our actions, but all of this emerges out of God's love and justice, not God's wrath.

I understand that not everyone will be comfortable with this kind of radical revisioning of how we as Christians can read the Bible, but I am convinced that Augustine's idea that the Bible can be interpreted in many different ways simply makes more sense than a more brittle idea that verses in Scripture can only have one correct meaning. A mystical approach to Scripture holds the idea that the Bible is meant to guide us in our relationship with God but not to suppress us into submission to just "one correct" way of reading it. This liberates us to see the Bible as a sacred book in conversation with itself, and it allows us to see how other inspiring and learned commentators (like Julian of Norwich and many other mystics) offer us insight into how to read the Bible as well. Of course, Julian—like anyone else—may have made mistakes, or gotten some things wrong. We are not required to slavishly obey everything she (or anyone else) says about the text.

We need to bring critical thinking and adult discernment to bear when we read the Bible (or, for that matter, when we read biblical scholars, commentators, and interpreters). We can be assured that we will not always agree with the experts or each other, and we have to be humble enough to admit that we ourselves don't always get it right either.

When we see the Bible as more like a conversation than a monologue, then we who read the Bible today are invited to join in an ongoing conversation that has already been continuing for centuries and will carry on long after we are gone. We need to do so humbly, acknowledging that we don't have all the answers. But when a writer says something that rings true, it's worth taking it on, at least as a hypothesis.

For me, Julian's declaration that there's no wrath in God absolutely rings true. When I hear Christians talk about the wrath of God, I assume they are telling me more about themselves and *their* beliefs and image of God than offering me anything new about the God who is vast, limitless love and compassion.

I think Julian's words represent an important and profound spiritual statement. Julian is calling us to a more consistent and hopeful understanding of God as infinitely loving, infinitely compassionate, infinitely merciful. To do this, we must learn new ways of interpreting the Bible. But the good news is that we can continue to read the Bible as an inspiring text while also taking into consideration the wisdom of all the ages in learning how to interpret it most consistently and most lovingly.

*   *   *

Read the Bible like Saint Ignatius of Loyola

St. Ignatius (1491–1556) was a founder of the Society of Jesus (the Jesuits) and, in terms of mysticism, is most noted for being the author of the *Spiritual Exercises*, an in-depth retreat experience designed to cultivate a deepening one-on-one relationship with Christ—fostered through the spiritual imagination. The spiritual exercises can be done intensively over a thirty-day period or as a daily spiritual practice within everyday life that can take eight months or more. It is a rich and rewarding spiritual process—and at its heart, it invites us to use our imaginative capacity for prayer, meditation, reading the Bible, and seeking greater intimacy with God through Christ.

So to read the Bible like Ignatius, use your imagination. Imagine yourself as if you were present in whatever story you are reading. Then the story truly comes alive within your imagination and offers you a richer sense of the impact that particular story could have on your life (I offer some more insight into Ignatian prayer, which pairs quite well with *lectio divina* for the contemplative approach to Scripture, in the appendix).

*   *   *

Read the Bible like Saint Teresa of Ávila

Like Hildegard and Julian, Teresa is known more for her deep spirituality than for being a Bible scholar—it's important to remember that in the Middle Ages and the Renaissance, women did not have access to the educational resources that were reserved for men. But even without a formal education, Teresa was a brilliant mystic and a gifted writer, and her spirituality was built around a deeply intimate sense that Christ was both her *lord* and also her *beloved*. That's the key to reading the Bible in the spirit of Teresa: read it as a love story and interpret every verse and passage in terms of "how does this help me to be more intimate with God?" Like many mystics throughout history, Teresa loved the Song of Songs, the beautiful sensual and even erotic love poem found in the wisdom literature of the Hebrew Scriptures—and widely seen as a metaphor for God's love for both Israel and the Christian Church but also Christ's compassionate love for each of us as individuals. To read the Bible like Teresa, approach it like a delicious love story where you are one of the main "lovers," responding to the infinite desire of the Divine.

* * *

Read the Bible like Howard Thurman

Moving into the twentieth century, one of the great mystics of our time was Howard Thurman (1899–1981), the grandson of slaves who became a Baptist minister, a mentor to Martin Luther King Jr., and one of the great voices of our time calling for the integration of justice (action) and spirituality (contemplation). In books like *Jesus and the Disinherited* and *Meditations of the Heart*, Thurman demonstrates how his love for the Bible (and for the life of faith in general) is always about integrating the inner consent to divine love with the outer commitment to live out the faith by working to make the world a better, more just, and more humane place. Thurman reminds us that we do not read the Bible merely for our own private, interior edification; the life of the mystic is the life of one who washes the feet of those who are in need or suffer—from those who are hungry, sick, or imprisoned to those who struggle under the weight of injustice, oppression, and the lack of privilege.

*   *   *

Read the Bible like Pauli Murray

Murray (1910–1985), like Howard Thurman, is renowned for her commitment to social justice and the struggle for freedom and liberation. Although recognized as a spiritual leader— she was the first woman of color to be ordained an Episcopal priest—she never, to the best of my knowledge, claimed to be a mystic or has been called that by others. But in the spirit of every person being a special kind of mystic, Murray can be an inspiration for us, if for no other reason than this one comment that reveals her spiritually informed way of reading the Bible: "Our concern is not with the historical accuracy of the details, but with the religious truth these stories represent." Ironically, she said this in the context of a sermon on the story of Hagar in Genesis 21: the same passage that Saint Paul inter- prets in Galatians 4. With her words, Murray is not dismissing the importance of good scholarship (or good history); she is reminding us that a spiritual reading of the Bible involves more than just an academic understanding. As a woman, a woman of color, and very likely a genderqueer person (some scholars believe she may have been what we now describe as nonbinary), Pauli Murray reminds us that Christian spirituality—and the Bible—is for all people, not just those who historically have had access to social power and privilege. She invites us to read the Bible from a place of radical solidarity with all people.

*   *   *

Read the Bible like Desmond Tutu

During his long life, South African archbishop Desmond Tutu (1931–2021) was another spiritual leader best known for his tireless work for justice and equality, especially in terms of dismantling the evil of Apartheid. But Archbishop Tutu's deep intimacy with God shone through his life and ministry, not the least of which in his decades-long friendship with the Tibetan Buddhist leader, His Holiness the XIVth Dalai Lama. His biographer Michael Battle highlights Tutu's mysticism as a defining theme of the archbishop's life. So this particular mystic adds yet another layer to our Bible-reading toolbox: to read the Christian sacred text with a heart open to the wisdom and compassion found in other faiths. In his book *God Is Not a Christian*, Tutu makes the following comment about interfaith spirituality in general, but it also serves as a great principle for how we encounter the Bible: "We must be ready to learn from one another, not claiming that we alone possess all truth and that somehow we have a corner on God." So to read the Bible like this particular mystic means not only to seek intimacy with God, inspiration for the ongoing struggle for justice, and nurturing of a spirituality immersed in joy, but it also recognizes that the wisdom of those who are different from ourselves—even including those who come from different religious and spiritual traditions—can be an essential resource for helping us to go deeper in our own engagement with the sacred text of our (or any) tradition.

*   *   *

Read the Bible like Richard Rohr

Born in 1943, Richard Rohr—founder of the Center for Action and Contemplation and a beloved teacher of visionary spirituality—is still alive as of this writing; I wanted to include at least one living mystic to emphasize that mystics are not just figures of the past (although I suspect it would embarrass him to be labeled a mystic, such is his humility). Rohr is beloved in our time as a spiritual teacher and an inspiration not only to Christians but to people who feel alienated from institutional religion or who find spiritual sustenance from other faiths besides, or in addition to, Christianity. As a lifelong Catholic and a Franciscan priest, Rohr himself is steeped in the wisdom of the Bible (his career as a public speaker began with an audiobook series he did on the "Great Themes" of both the Old and New Testaments). Unlike most of the mystics profiled in this chapter, Rohr is like Origen in that he has written specifically about how to read the Bible spiritually.

His books *Things Hidden: Scripture as Spirituality* and *What Do We Do with the Bible?* are essential resources for anyone seeking an authentically mystical relationship with Scripture. In *Things Hidden*, Rohr emphasizes many of these themes I've touched on in this book: reading Scripture as the expression of a loving relationship between God and humanity, looking at the difficult texts as "bad examples" of how *not* to be spiritual, and trusting that the entire story of the Bible is like any great romance—it has plot twists and setbacks, but the overall message is one of ever-deepening intimacy with the Source of Love. *What Do We Do with the Bible?* is a short book, only available directly from the Center for Action and Contemplation; it makes a powerful statement about reading Scripture: that the consciousness we bring to the Bible will determine what we get out of it. In other words, if you read the Bible *as* a mystic, you will find the mystical wisdom encoded within it, but if you insist on reading it dualistically or even like a fundamentalist, then you will probably just be caught up in the passages that seem to promote God as a patriarchal figure who metes out rewards and punishments. That principle from Brian McLaren, "What you focus on determines what you miss," seems to apply here. So one of the best ways to find the mysticism within the Bible is to work on cultivating our own mystical hearts—not just through reading the Bible or any other book of spiritual wisdom but through cultivating a practice of prayer, meditation, contemplation, and the loving service of others. To read like a mystic, become a mystic.

*   *   *

These twelve mystics, ranging from the New Testament to the present day, represent only a small fraction of the many great contemplatives and mystics to have found spiritual sustenance from reading the Bible and who, in their own writings and teachings, have left us clues for how we can do the same. But even among these twelve, we find great diversity—which is just a reminder that there is no one right way to read the Bible like a mystic. Read the Bible to help yourself fall more deeply in love with the Spirit of Love, and then you, too, will read the Bible not only like a mystic but *as* a mystic.

*   *   *

7

Purification, Illumination, Union, and Beyond

But as the study of physical life is made easier for us by an artificial division into infancy, adolescence, maturity, and old age, so a discreet indulgence of the human passion for map-making will increase our chances of understanding the nature of the Mystic Way.

—Evelyn Underhill

* * *

IN THIS CHAPTER, I want to expand on Richard Rohr's idea that the level of consciousness we bring to the Bible will determine what our experience of reading it will be like. To discover the mystical wisdom in the Bible, we need to bring a mystical sensibility to how we read Scripture. There is a kind of chicken-and-egg dynamic at play here: to foster our own mystical spirituality, the wisdom of the Bible can help us tremendously. My point is *not* that you have to become a great mystic like Teresa of Ávila or Meister Eckhart before you can dare to try to read the Bible. We start where we are. But when you bring to the Bible a desire to become a mystic or to grow in the mystical life, the Bible can inspire you along the way.

*   *   *

Origen of Alexandria's contribution to mystical Christianity does not end with his three ways of reading Scripture. He also developed the classical understanding of how mystical spirituality evolves over the course of a single lifespan. A complete human lifetime involves a series of ages beginning with infancy, then childhood, the tween years, adolescence, young adulthood, prime adulthood, the middle-age years, and on to maturity and eventually old age. These stages or ages of life correspond to ordinary physical growth and development—the body of a ten-year-old is considerably different from the body of a fifty-year-old—and there are intellectual, emotional, social, and psychological stages that humans progress through, which may or may not correspond to our physical life changes. When all goes well, we expect people to mature psychologically just like we do physically; this is why we praise a child who acts grown-up for their age but criticize a forty-year-old who is said to act like a "big baby."

The spiritual life has its own itinerary of growth, development, and changes. Emory University professor James Fowler wrote a classic study called *Stages of Faith*, where he identified seven phases of spiritual growth and change that a person could experience over their lifetime. Of course, just as a person can sometimes die too young or never manage to become a mature adult even if they live many years, so, too, is no one guaranteed that they will make it through to all seven of Fowler's stages. But the theory holds that if a person lives a full life and follows their spiritual journey in the context of a basically healthy faith community and personal growth, then they will likely experience all the stages over the course of their years. Fowler's stages are similar to Erik Erikson's stages of psychosocial development or Jean Piaget's theory of cognitive development.

Back to Origen—while he did not develop as complex a model as Fowler's seven stages of faith, he did theorize that the mystical life involves a series of three stages of inner growth and development. His model became deeply influential over the course of Christian history; scholars are still commenting on Origen's ideas to this day. What's interesting for our purposes is that Origen drew his inspiration from the Bible—particularly the wisdom literature of the Hebrew Scriptures—to illustrate his three-stage map for spiritual growth. In doing so, Origen appeals to Scripture as if to say, "My ideas about spirituality are mirrored in the very way the Bible is organized."

*   *   *

Here's a brief description of Origen's three stages of mystical growth and development, presented along with the book of the Bible that illustrates each stage. The stages are identified as *purification, illumination,* and *union.* We'll look at how each of these stages of the inner life offers us insight into how to read the Bible mystically.

* * *

Purification

The starting point of the spiritual life, at least from the perspective of classical Christian mysticism, is a process of *purification* (sometimes also called *purgation*). This stage begins with the assumption that most of us have plenty of spiritual wounds, addictions, bad habits, or just plain character flaws that we need to either heal or let go of. In classical religious language, we are all sinners, and the first step in spiritual life is repenting (turning away from) our sins. Unfortunately, that language is deeply problematic. For example, it is so important to remember that addiction is an illness, not a moral failing, even though the consequences of addiction often involve actions that cause harm to self and others. It's tragic how the language of sin and repentance, which is meant to help us heal, has been weaponized to shame people (especially those who are judged by the standards of authoritarian or fundamentalist religion as being inherently fallen or immoral) since in the dualistic eyes of legalistic religion, there is only one right way to be moral or righteous. Because of this abuse of spiritual teachings, I would recommend that we think of this stage not in terms of *repenting from sin* but rather in terms of *recovery* from all the ways we avoid, resist, or sabotage love in our lives and in our relationships.

Historically, sin was understood as an offense against God; since the Bible clearly states that God is love, perhaps the most useful and meaningful way of thinking about sin is anything we say, think, or do that alienates us from love, including love for God, love for others, love for ourselves, and love for creation. Love can never be a sin, for God is love—which is why the church's hostility to queer people is such a betrayal of God; what right does the church have to tell anyone who they can or cannot love? Of course, we can betray love when we relate to others in harmful ways (e.g., being abusive, or stalking, or violating preexisting relationship boundaries), but love itself is never wrong.

The stage of purification corresponds to the book of Proverbs in the wisdom literature of the Hebrew Scriptures. Proverbs is a collection of maxims and pithy sayings all designed to help a person live a decent and ethical life. In light of today's knowledge, especially psychology and sociology, we might argue with some of the philosophical, ethical, or theological assumptions behind the book of Proverbs, but the basic idea is timeless: we human beings sometimes need help to guide us to making wise and loving choices in our ethics and behavior. Such, then, is the first stage of the mystical life.

Another analogy here comes from the recovery movement. In a twelve-step program, a person seeking to recover from alcoholism or some other dependency goes through a process of acknowledging that their addiction has caused harm: it has directly or indirectly resulted in behaviors where relationships, careers, and families are hurt or even destroyed because of the actions of the addicted person. Part of the recovery process is taking a "fearless moral inventory" of one's self, acknowledging as honestly as possible the exact nature of one's harmful acts; then admitting all this to one's self, to God, and to another person; and then asking God for healing so that such behaviors could cease and following up, where possible, by making amends to those who had been hurt (including, of course, one's own self).

I've just described steps 3–10 of the 12-step program, literally two-thirds of the entire program, and this is very similar to what the mystical stage of purification is like.

*   *   *

Illumination

We never fully heal from our capacity to create suffering and harm and to alienate ourselves from love. The human capacity to make wrong or foolish choices seems never to go away, not even among saints. In other words, we never fully graduate from the stage of purification. Nevertheless, as we mature in taking responsibility for living a life oriented toward love rather than toward selfishness, narcissism, or abuse (or trapped within the illness of addiction), we open our hearts and souls to the gift of the second stage of the mystical life: the state of *illumination*, which corresponds to the wisdom book of Ecclesiastes. The logic here is beautifully simple: remove the obstacles to love, and love itself will come flooding into our lives, and we will experience such Divine Love as a kind of inward radiance—an illumination of the spirit.

This is similar to the concept of enlightenment found in Eastern spiritualities, although the Western concept of illumination is much more down-to-earth and accessible than the way enlightenment is sometimes depicted. Read the story of the Buddha's enlightenment, and it seems like he suddenly became infinitely knowledgeable about all things (this is a theme that shows up in different mythologies from around the world, for example, in the Celtic myth of Taliesin, the Welsh bard who tasted a potion that afforded him godlike powers of knowledge and skill). We can safely assume that such elevated language is hyperbolic, a kind of spiritual tall tale that many people find inspiring or challenging and is no more literally true than Jesus walking on the water but nevertheless speaks to a real and meaningful experience, even if only an experience in our spiritual imagination. Seen in a more down-to-earth (humbler) way, illumination or enlightenment represents the manifestation of true wisdom and compassion in our lives.

Ecclesiastes is one of the more fascinating books in the Bible; some people find it rather existential or even cynical in its "eat, drink, and be merry, for tomorrow we die" approach to life. I think Origen was drawn to it because he saw it as an expression of Solomon's wisdom (traditionally, King Solomon was thought to be the author of Ecclesiastes), and so if mystical illumination equals the attainment of wisdom, then a book that expresses the wisdom of a great king was, for Origen, an excellent symbol of this stage of the mystical life. What I think is important for us to remember is that mystical illumination is not only about becoming truly wise but also truly loving, which is to say *compassionate*. But that also sets the stage for the third and highest stage of the mystical life.

*   *   *

Union

Like purification, enlightenment is not something we ever fully master and then move beyond. A life shaped by wisdom and compassion (and the joy and felicity that naturally accompany a well-lived life) is something we all would hope to enjoy for the duration of our earthly life, but mystical spirituality is about more than just living a good and happy life, no matter how attractive and appealing that may be. According to Origen, the summit of mystical living is the stage of *union* as exemplified by the Song of Songs. This stage is also called the *unitive life* or (in Greek) *theosis* or (in Latin) *deification*. The key to this stage is union with God.

The Song of Songs is one of the shortest and loveliest books in the entire Bible; on the surface, it is simply a passionate, even erotic love poem between a bride and her groom.

The language is earthy and sensual, and while the ancient authors never come right out and say so, anyone who reads this imaginatively comes to see that the love in this relationship is shaped by desire, yearning, ecstasy, and yes, physical intimacy. Many biblical commentators over the centuries have seemed a little nonplussed by the unashamed sexiness of this poem, but it's part of the Bible, so who can criticize it? What the commentators have done, however, is interpret it as an allegory: the bride and groom represent Israel and God, or the church and Jesus, or—for the mystics—the bride is each individual person, called into a profoundly intimate and deeply loving (and satisfying) relationship with Christ, with God.

So the mysticism of union is the mysticism of love—not just love embodied as compassion that we share with each other but the fountain of ecstatic, mystical love that can only flow between human and divine. God is love, and so God loves each of us: joyfully, sensually, ecstatically, unconditionally. And we are free either to resist or reject that love (which would be a bummer) or to accept that love's claim on our hearts, thereby consenting to let Divine Love flow in us and through us, transforming us into the fullness of God's very image and likeness, stamped on our souls. If we say yes to the love of God in our lives, we become transformed by that love, to the point of being made one with it, so that we become the very embodied manifestation of Divine Love in human form. Many mystics use profound and deeply poetic language to describe union with love in terms of the disappearance of the self, the experience of no boundaries between "I" and "God," a sense of blissful beatitude where God and I are not-two.

If that sounds pretty exalted, well, that's what mysticism promises us. This is far beyond just "be a good person and go to heaven when you die"—that kind of religiosity, so prevalent in the institutional church, is like spirituality stuck at the purification stage: a kind of mystical arrested development. Mysticism, at its heart, recognizes that spirituality is about so much more than just learning how to be a moral or ethical person (as worthy as that may be): in the words of Trappist author Michael Casey, "Christian life consists not so much in being good as in becoming God." Of course it matters to embody *goodness*, but it goes so much deeper than just being "moral" (especially given how traditional ideas of morality have been misused and weaponized against "outsiders," such as unbelievers, and followers of other religions). We can criticize the classical ideas around morality and still accept that spirituality involves living consciously, ethically, and with a commitment to justice, kindness, compassion, and care—and the mystics remind us that the promise of visionary spirituality is to grow from conscious living to *divinized* loving: being one with the God of love.

Like we never fully graduate from the stages of purification and illumination, in a similar way, no one ever fully masters the life of union. Many Christian mystics have tried to put this into words: for example, in Teresa of Ávila's *The Interior Castle*, the final "mansion" of the mystical castle is Teresa's attempt to explain what the unitive life might be like. But we run into a problem: most mystics feel that this joyful summation of mystical attainment simply cannot be contained by language or even by human thought, so therefore any attempt to write about it ultimately fails, not because the mystic is unworthy but because no tongue can express the splendor of divine union.

*   *   *

On beyond Union

Origen's map of the mystical life has endured for over 1,500 years, providing a meaningful guideline for many spiritual seekers, generation after generation. But it is not the only model for mystical living; other mystics and thinkers have developed other ways of describing the mystical life—most famously Saint Teresa of Ávila, author of *The Interior Castle*, which describes spiritual growth using the metaphor of a tour through seven mansions within a giant castle. Her compatriot, Saint John of the Cross, used the metaphor of a dark night to describe periods of intense inner transformation and letting go as a way of growing into deeper union with God; John himself spoke of two different dark nights, the dark night of the senses and the dark night of the soul. In our time, Cynthia Bourgeault (following the wisdom of recent mystics like Thomas Keating and Bernadette Roberts) has recognized a third dark night, the dark night of the self. And Evelyn

Underhill, in her classic 1911 study of mysticism, integrates the ideas of Origen and John of the Cross to map her own five-stage model of the mystical life: awakening, purification, illumination, dark night, and the unitive life.

Over the past century, another word for attempting to describe the heart of the mystical life has emerged, *nonduality*—borrowed from Eastern philosophy and brought into Christian wisdom by interspiritual pioneers like Bede Griffiths, Sara Grant, Abhishiktananda, and Bruno Barnhart. It's a challenging term to define (Cynthia Bourgeault does a wonderful job of deconstructing what it *doesn't* mean in her book *The Heart of Centering Prayer*), but for our purposes, we could say it points to an experiential recognition of the foundational unity to all things that is deeper and more real than the apparent dualities and multiplicities that meet the eye—culminating in the ultimate unity, the union separating any distinction between God and God's beloved creation. Along these lines, some contemplative teachers—from Meister Eckhart to Cynthia Bourgeault—have suggested that the ongoing efflorescence of the mystical life implies that even the exalted language of union (unitive life) might be inadequate to fully chart such phenomena as the experience of the death/dissolution of the ego, the nondual awareness where even categories such as *consciousness* and *self* and *relationship* fall away, leaving only the pure beingness of oneness with the mystery. As I write these words, they feel clunky and awkward—I am trying to invite us into a sense of the omega point of mysticism, but that takes us so far off the scale of ordinary human experience that all words, all concepts, all maps begin to lose their reference points and efficacy. There, only the pure love and deep guidance of the Spirit can truly guide us, but mystics again and again invite us into that deep and wondrous place.

*   *   *

Bringing the Map of the Mystical Life to the Bible (and Vice Versa)

"A map is not the territory it represents," noted philosopher Alfred Korzybski, "but, if correct, it has a similar structure to the territory, which accounts for its usefulness." Every human being is a special kind of mystic, so any map of the interior life will always be imperfect, and no model of the spiritual life will work for everyone. My purpose in writing this book is not to provide you a detailed map of mysticism in the Bible; not only do I humbly feel that I cannot create such a map (I am still a mere learner, still discovering the unitive treasures in Scripture for myself), but I also believe that anyone and everyone is more likely to discover mystical depth in reading Scripture if their only and final guide is the Spirit at work in their own heart. In other words, any particular teaching or passage in the Bible may be thrumming with contemplative wisdom, but for whatever reason, many readers (including you and me) simply don't see it when we read that particular passage. This, I believe, is because the Spirit reveals wisdom to us when we are ready to receive it—so if I tried to give you a list of all the "mystical" passages in the Bible, the list would really only be a compendium of all the verses and passages that have shimmered with celestial insight *for me*. If you really must know, here are nine verses or passages that have been especially meaningful for my own faith journey: Psalm 65:1 (but find an accurate translation or read it in the Hebrew if you can; most English translations get this one wrong), the Song of Songs, Ecclesiastes 3:11, much of the Sermon on the Mount (Matthew 5–7), John 15:4–11, Romans 5:5, Ephesians 3, 2 Peter 1:2–4, and 1 John 4:7–19. Of course, there are many more.

You may read those same passages and scratch your head, wondering what all the fuss was about. Meanwhile, other stories or teachings in the Bible are ready for you to discover for yourself—but if you are busy just trying to follow up on all of *my* contemplative passages, you could miss the treasure waiting for you.

* * *

So with the disclaimer in mind, for the rest of this chapter, I want to give you not an exhaustive list (again, I don't think that's really possible) but a few ideas to get you started. My suggestion is that when you read any passage in the Bible, ask yourself questions like these: Does this passage offer me insight and encouragement for my ongoing journey of personal *purification*? Or does it encourage me to embrace and celebrate the *illumination* that only comes to our hearts through the Holy Spirit? Or does it invite me to consent to the divine gift of *union* that I could never manifest by my own will but can only allow to emerge in my life through the gift of divine grace?

Questions like these will give you the capacity to look for mystical insight in Scripture that may be especially relevant to you and where you are in your spiritual life today. A passage that may open up entirely new insights or experiences of God today may not carry the same impact when you read it five years ago (or read it five years from now). The Spirit always seeks to meet us in the present—the here and now. Remember, your spiritual imagination is the key to accessing the mystical wisdom in the Bible (or, indeed, in any book). Imagine what the Spirit wants *you* to discern, recognize, intuit, understand, and consent to as you read any given passage. From there, it's all between you and the Spirit.

*   *   *

Reading the Bible for Insight into Inner Growth and Transformation

Purification is a concept that many Christians have used aggressively, especially toward girls and women (think of purity rings), so it might be a word you find triggering or problematic. I would recommend replacing it with *inner growth and transformation*. The mystical path begins with taking responsibility for living a conscious, mindful, conscientious, and compassionate life. In the words of Spike Lee, it's about "doing the right thing"—for God, for ourselves, and for our communities. The Bible has a deserved reputation as a treasury of ethical wisdom and challenges for us (both individually and communally) to be the best we can be. This is not just about being moral but about living well as we get started on the spiritual path.

- *The Ten Commandments (Exodus 20:2–17, Deuteronomy 5:6–21)*—The central moral precepts of the Hebrew Scriptures—and, therefore, foundational to the New Testament as well—is this code of ten nonnegotiable rules, said to have been given to Moses directly from God. Taken as a whole, the commandments provide a succinct statement of what lines *not* to cross when seeking to live a good life: do not lie, do not steal, do not overwork, do not let jealousy or unrestrained desire sabotage your relationships. Mystics understand that spirituality is about something far deeper than just following the rules, but you have to walk before you can run, and the first steps for living a mystical life is learning to bring integrity and conscientiousness to the conduct of our lives. Even if you may quibble with the details, overall the commandments mark out the starting point of any serious spiritual practice.

- *The Beatitudes (Matthew 5:1–12)*—What the commandments were to Moses, the Beatitudes are to Jesus; they do not replace the commandments but deepen their ethical challenge. Jesus is less interested in what limits to enforce and more concerned with the positive marks that shape a good life—what he identifies as "blessed" (which has also been translated as *happy*). Be merciful, seek justice, foster peace, live humbly, be spiritually unencumbered. We live in an age that is allergic to moral mandates, but if we allow these principles to challenge us to grow, we will walk far along the path of growth and transformation.

- *The Fruit of the Spirit (Galatians 5:22–23)*—Imagine that the commandments are like soil and the beatitudes are seeds planted therein. Take care of those seeds, and eventually they will mature and bear fruit. This list of virtues and qualities from the apostle Paul is not so much a to-do list for the life of inner transformation but rather a guide to what you can expect to see manifest in your life as you mature in your faith. What's the point of doing all the kind of self-improvement that this stage entails if it doesn't foster love, peace, and joy in your life? And those are only the first three of the nine fruits listed here.

- *The Book of Proverbs (representative passage: Proverbs 8:1–21)*—I've known dedicated Christians who

grumble that the book of Proverbs is overly patriarchal and legalistic, and frankly I think they have
a point. As I have been saying all along, one of the
keys to reading the Bible well is being willing to
argue with it when needed. Nevertheless, this was
the book that inspired Origen to suggest that the
first act of the spiritual life is inner transformation,
and in between the cringey stuff are some inspiring
passages like the "hymn to wisdom" found in chapter 8. From King Solomon to the Buddha, there's a
cross-cultural understanding that spiritual maturity
fosters wisdom; at its best, Proverbs encourages us to
make wisdom a priority and a goal for our lives.

- *The Prophets (representative verses: Hosea 12:6, Micah
  6:8, Amos 5:24)*—Forget the secular idea that prophecy is about foretelling the future; in the Hebrew
  Bible, the prophets are simply those who speak for
  God, and their messages are usually aimed at the
  moment in which they lived; in other words, divine
  prophecy speaks of God not for the future but for
  the present. Their present may be our past, but much
  of their wisdom continues to both challenge and
  inspire spiritual seekers today. The three verses I've
  highlighted are some of the most famous moral/eth-
  ical precepts in the entire Bible (and proof positive
  that the Hebrew Scriptures are every bit as spiritually
  advanced as the New Testament), but they are just

the tip of the proverbial iceberg. Read the prophets for personal inspiration and also for a clear message of social responsibility and the mandate to foster justice for all.

*　*　*

Reading the Bible for Insight into Illumination

When you clean a dirty window, more light shines through. As we take responsibility for removing the dust and grime of our unloving and uncaring actions from our lives, it only makes sense that we will begin to discover a divine light shining within us (and through us). It's not a reward for being good; it's simply an ability to finally see what has always been there. People who recover from a cigarette addiction are blown away at how much better their sense of smell becomes—actually, it's just being restored to what it was meant to be all along. The mystical stage of illumination operates much the same way. Many of the stories and images in the Bible that call us into illumination are obviously mythological, but they often invite us to consider that the Spirit of Love, residing in our hearts, can immerse us in uncreated light—all we have to do is consent to it.

- *The Burning Bush (Exodus 3)*—Before he liberated the people of Israel from their enslavement in Egypt (and went on to receive the Ten Commandments), Moses began his heroic journey with an otherworldly encounter with the voice of God in the wilderness, encountered through a bush that burned without being consumed. Ever since then, the spirit of God has been compared to metaphorical fire: a fire that, likewise, burns within our hearts and yet empowers us to give away its light. If *you* ran into a burning bush, what would you do? And what do you think the voice of God would ask of you?

- *Jacob wrestling with God (Genesis 32:22–32)*— Moses's ancestor Jacob spent a night outdoors by the ford of a river, where a stranger wrestled him until dawn. The stranger refuses to reveal their name and instead gives Jacob a new name: Israel. It's a mysterious and even unsettling story, but it reminds us that sometimes our encounter with God is suffused with mystery and unanswered questions. Sometimes God comes to us in the darkness, wrestles with us, refuses to answer our questions, but will nevertheless bless us. Here we see the beginning of a recurring theme among mystics: sometimes the "light of the world" comes to us in darkness, so mystical illumination is bigger than just the presence of light. The moral of the story: always assume that God may show up at any time and in any circumstance. No situation is beyond the movement of the Spirit.

- *Isaiah's vision (Isaiah 6)*—The book of Isaiah is the longest of the Bible's prophetic writings (and involves the words of at least three different prophets). The story of how the first Isaiah receives his vocation (his calling to be a prophet) is certainly dramatic: a vision of God in God's temple, surrounded by angels, filled with smoke (I like to imagine it as incense) and thundering with the chanting of the angel's praise. It reminds me of what I learned in college about Shakespeare's plays: he would begin a play with ghosts or witches or something else equally dramatic, basically to get the attention of the audience (audiences in Shakespeare's day were pretty rowdy). Wouldn't God send us something dramatic (like a vision of angels and smoke and fire) to get *our* attention? Well, not always, but this story reminds us that when God has something to say to us, perhaps we'd be wise to shut up and listen.

- *Ecclesiastes (representative passage: Ecclesiastes 3:1– 14)*—Origen links the stage of illumination to the book of Ecclesiastes, which just might be the most cynical book in the Bible ("there is nothing new under the sun") but which is seen as a repository of King Solomon's wisdom (in truth, we don't know who actually wrote Ecclesiastes, but historically Solomon got the credit). If Proverbs represents the idea that a conscious life points us toward wisdom, Ecclesiastes is meant to illustrate that yes, wisdom will come to those who seek it. Like the story of Jacob, Ecclesiastes reminds us that the "illumination" of this stage of mystical living is perhaps best understood metaphorically: it is the light that enlightens our wisdom (which is a prelude to the even brighter light of love that the stage of union represents).

- *The Nativity and the Epiphany (Matthew 1–2, Luke 1–2)*—The word *epiphany* literally means *manifestation* and refers to the visitation of the magi—the three kings or wise men of Christmas legend. In the gospels of Matthew and Luke, the stories about the birth of Jesus are very different (in popular culture, we tend to mash them together when celebrating Christmas each December), but the common thread in both versions is that with the birth of Jesus, the very Son of God has been made manifest among us humans. Perhaps this is the heart of mystical illumination: we seek the manifestation of the Spirit in our hearts the way the magi sought the manifestation of the divine in a baby born in a stable. When I was a teenager, I heard a preacher complete a sermon on Christmas by saying, "What really matters is how Jesus is being born in *our* hearts today"; I didn't know it at the time, but this is a recurring message among the mystics. In the words of the twentieth-century British mystic Caryll Houselander, "The one thing that we all have to do [is] to bear Christ into the world." Do not seek the light of illumination from without you; seek it within, and if passages in the Bible like the ones I've listed here can help you recognize that inner light, then they have done their purpose, and you have read them like a mystic.

*   *   *

Reading the Bible for Insight into Union

Origen's final stage for the mystical life is the stage of union (or the unitive life, or theosis, deification, divinization). While mystics and contemplatives in our time are suggesting that even the stage of union is not the final endpoint (can there ever be a final endpoint when it comes to union with God?), it's still a handy marker for identifying verses and passages in the Bible that inspire us to recognize our already existing (but often deeply hidden) status as beings who are one with the divine. This is not something any of us can effectively put into words, so as you read the passages I've suggested, you might not get the same intuition of the presence of God from them that I do. If that's the case, my suggestion is that you will encounter the face of God in other passages more quickly than in these. The Spirit is shy, and the presence of the sacred is alluded to, rather than explicitly proclaimed, in many passages throughout Scripture. Look for the thrill of recognition: does any passage you read dare you to wonder, hope, believe that God is already closer to you than you are to yourself? If a passage strikes you that way, pause, take a breath, and linger there and savor the wisdom. If you are seeking God, you are simply responding to God's desire to be found. Many words and verses and entire sections of the Bible can support you on the way.

- *The Still Small Voice (1 Kings 19:11–12)*—When Elijah the prophet is on the run from a hostile queen, he hides out in the mountains, and the Spirit calls him to step out from his cave. In quick succession, he encounters a powerful wind, an earthquake, and a fire but finds God in none of these. Instead, he finds God in a "still small voice" or a "light silent sound" or "the sound of sheer silence" (different English Bibles translate this verse in different ways). It's kind of the inverse of Isaiah 6: meeting God not in the drama but in *silence*. And while the passage doesn't say it out loud, I think it's reasonable to assume that the still small voice comes from within. It's certainly *heard* within.
- *The Song of Songs (representative passage: 2:1–14)*— The third book used by Origen to illustrate the dynamic from purification to illumination to union, the Song of Songs is a deliciously sensual and beautiful love poem. Lyrical and dramatic, and in places frankly erotic (much of which gets lost in translation),

this is the ground zero of the overriding metaphor in Christian mysticism that union between God and human is like the blissful union of two spouses in a happy marriage. In traditional Christian weddings we hear something to the effect of "the two shall become one" (quoting Jesus from the Sermon on the Mount); this is the principle underlying the Song of Songs, which works equally well as a simple and straightforward love poem and a description of mystical union.

- *The Transfiguration (Matthew 17:1–8, Mark 9:2–8, Luke 9:28–36)*—This is a dramatic story where Jesus takes three of his closest friends to the top of Mount Tabor and then is "transfigured" before them. Jesus becomes radiant with light (illumination taken to the nth degree!), the voice of God is heard, and even two great figures from the Hebrew Scriptures, Moses and Elijah, show up for a chat. Peter, James, and John are amazed and don't know what to say (in one of the Gospels, Peter babbles on about building "booths" for the three shining figures; it seems pretty obvious to me that Peter is freaking out and blurting out the first thing that pops into his head). It's a powerful and imaginative way of underscoring the basic Christian idea that Jesus is one with God. Pair that with what he says in the farewell discourse, and the core message of mysticism is revealed.

- *The Farewell Discourse (John 15:1–17)*—Four chapters in the Gospel of John are devoted to the farewell discourse, which is the talk Jesus gives to his followers the night before he was killed. If the Sermon on the Mount represents the foundation of Jesus's public teaching, the farewell discourse is the final summation of his teachings, especially meant for his closest followers (but you and I get included as well). "Abide in me as I abide in you," proclaims the one who was filled with light on Mount Tabor. He makes it clear that when we human beings love one another, we are manifesting Christ (and the Spirit) in our hearts: we are one with the one who is one with God.

- *The Third Heaven (2 Corinthians 12:2–4)*—Don't think Jesus is the only one who gets to have nondual fun in the New Testament. In his second letter to the faith community of Corinth, Paul tells a story about someone who was "caught up to the third heaven" (Paul tells the story in the third person, but many scholars assume he is speaking about himself). What does he mean by *third heaven*? It has been speculated that the first heaven is the sky, the second heaven is outer space, so therefore the third heaven must be the actual dwelling place of God. That's based on a premodern understanding of the cosmos, of course, but for our purposes, it's a poetic and imaginative way of Paul emphasizing what was implied in Jesus's life and message: you and I are not just spectators invited to watch Jesus enjoy divine union; it's a gift offered to us all.

*   *   *

As I've written out these brief invitations to different passages in the Bible, I feel I need to emphasize that the mystical life is not like a college curriculum, where you have to take classes in a particular order so that you may graduate. Purification, illumination, union, and nonduality (see below) are not so much steps on a ladder as dimensions that converge in that place where you and God are not-two. Language (and therefore writing) is necessarily linear, so I'm trying to express a nonlinear reality (mystical experience or wisdom) into a linear method of communication. You can't put the ocean in a teacup. Please just keep this in mind as you seek your own invitation into mystical love when you explore Scripture.

*   *   *

Nonduality in the Bible?

When it comes to looking for nondual mystical wisdom in the Bible, it's useful to keep in mind that nonduality is not a proposition to be taught (or refuted); rather, it is a dimension of spiritual consciousness that may be experienced but is not easily described. It's like looking for a subatomic particle that you can't see directly—all you can see is the evidence that points to its existence. Having said that, I do believe there is evidence for nondual mysticism in the Bible. Here are a few verses to get you started on your own search.

If I ascend to heaven, you are there; if I make my bed in Sheol, you are there (Psalm 139:8).

This is an important starting point for the search for nonduality in the Bible since it begins not with humankind but with God. This verse, in essence, reminds us that God is everywhere, even in Sheol, the realm of the dead (which, interestingly, is translated as *hell* in the King James Bible). The Divine is omnipresent: God is everywhere, even in life, even in death, even in heaven, even in hell. At least one major Christian mystic, Isaac of Syria, suggested that the fires of hell are actually the fires of God's love, which is experienced as "hellish" by those who choose to reject such love. It's a helpful way of seeing eternity that deconstructs the punitive idea of God tormenting the damned in the lake of fire: when we die, we all spend eternity immersed in the love of God; we may freely choose whether we experience that love as radiant light or as burning flame. But either way, we are all one in that love. Put another way, God is nondual (God loves all people equally), but it is us humans who filter the love of God dualistically, dividing ourselves into the worthy sheep and the reprobate goats. (This echoes Julian of Norwich's teaching that there is no such thing as wrath in God, but sometimes we experience God as wrathful because of the wrath that exists in our own hearts.)

Your eye is the lamp of your body. If your eye is single, your whole body is full of light; but if it is hurtful, your body is full of darkness (Luke 11:34).

Luke 11:34 is one of those verses (like Psalm 65:1) that gets mistranslated when rendered into English, perhaps because some biblical scholars simply don't get the koanlike contemplative meaning of the original text. So while the Greek of Luke 11:34 clearly points to the eyes as *single* or *hurtful*, you'll see translations rendering these words as *healthy, clear, good, unclouded,* or, my favorite, *sound* (if your eyes are sound, do your ears need to be clear?). When this verse is translated as *healthy* versus *unhealthy,* ironically it reinforces the very dualism that Jesus is subtly attacking here. To crack the meaning of this teaching, consider that the "single" eye is the eye that sees nondually. It's what Julian of Norwich called "the fullness of joy"—the eye that beholds God in all. This can be challenging to many spiritually minded people, for naturally those who yearn for God tend to be the type of folks who reject sin, eschew evil, and stand opposed to racism, sexism, abuse, violence, addiction, so on and so forth. But if we believe God is present everywhere—even in hell (Psalm 139:8)—then isn't it our job, as contemplatives, to behold God, who is everywhere, even present in the face of human evil, suffering, hatred, addiction, and abuse? This is not to say God condones or causes such things, only that God is compassionately present. Learning to see God's presence (to behold God in all) becomes a necessary step in the journey of transformation, of bringing light into the darkness. We human beings can try to alleviate the suffering in our world because we know God is present in all things. As Richard Rohr puts it, "Everything belongs," which is not the same thing as "anything goes." Nonduality is not an excuse for inaction in the face of injustice or suffering; it is human nature to change things because the cosmos itself is always changing. We get hungry; we look for food. We get tired; we seek rest. We get lonely; we reach out to connect with others. Likewise, when we encounter evil or sin, we work for healing and positive transformation. But nonduality means that God is present in all things.

> *You have heard that it was said, "You shall love your neighbor and hate your enemy." But I say to you, Love your enemies and pray for those who persecute you, so that you may be children of your Father in heaven; for he makes his sun rise on the evil and on the good, and sends rain on the righteous and on the unrighteous. For if you love those who love you, what reward do you have? Do not even the tax collectors do the same? And if you greet only your brothers and sisters, what more are you doing than others? Do not even the Gentiles do the same? Be perfect, therefore, as your heavenly Father is perfect. (Matthew 5:43–48)*

Jesus himself is speaking here about one of the most difficult teachings in the Gospel. How can we love our enemies?

Isn't it natural to hate one's enemies? If we tell someone who has been traumatized that they must love the ones who have hurt them, isn't that just adding shame to the trauma? These are challenging ethical questions, and I think it's important to see Jesus's teaching as a call to compassion and care, not shame or control. Jesus is challenging us to set aside the dualistic mind that divides the world into "good" (what benefits me) and "evil" (what harms me). Jesus calls us to see the world from God's perspective. When you stand on the North Pole, every direction is south. When you see the cosmos like God sees it, from God's point of view, everything you look at is imperfect—so your task is to love it all, just like God loves it. God loves the cosmos nondually. God doesn't love some people more than others. God didn't play favorites between Mother Teresa and, say, Osama bin Laden. God loves them all, totally, completely, fully, nondually. From our human vantage point, it is easy to see how Mother Teresa alleviated suffering, whereas Osama bin Laden created it, so naturally we honor Mother Teresa as a saint and revile bin Laden as a terrorist. But God, who is perfect (nondual), loves all alike. Again, this is a challenging teaching because loving your enemy does *not* mean giving them a free pass or pretending that the harm they may have caused doesn't matter. It's related to the Christian call for forgiveness—not in order to whitewash over suffering and trauma but to begin to do the necessary work of healing the harm that has taken place. A spirituality anchored in the nondual recognition of the limitlessness of Divine Love can equip us to work more effectively to do the important work of healing and repair, not only in our lives but also in the fabric of society at large.

There is no longer Jew or Greek, there is no longer slave or free, there is no longer male and female; for all of you are one in Christ Jesus (Galatians 3:28).

What is Paul saying here? Of course Jews remained Jews, and Greeks remained Greeks; there is no evidence of mass liberation of slaves in Christian society, and gender differences have not disappeared. Nonduality does not erase differences; rather, it transcends them by inviting us into that God vantage point, where we can "behold God in all" and learn to love all, the way God loves all. In the love of God, human-level distinctions like nationality, gender, or socioeconomic status simply lose their grip on us. They don't go away, but they lose their potency to create suffering and harm—at least as long as we remain vigilant in our unity with the mind of Christ.

> *Let the same mind be in you that was in Christ Jesus (Philippians 2:5).*
>
> *For who has known the mind of the Lord so as to instruct him? But we have the mind of Christ (1 Corinthians 2:16).*

What does it mean to "have the mind of Christ"? When Paul instructs us to "let this mind be in you," he goes on to sing about Christ, though equal with God, taking on humility and self-emptying (kenosis) to embrace humanity—even including a violent, undignified death by crucifixion. Paul seems to be saying, "If Christ, who is God, can take on the worst experience of being human, shouldn't we do the same?" The key is "the mind of Christ," which I believe is the mind of nondual consciousness. When we embrace the "everything belongs" mind in which we see all things with the eyes of God, loving with the heart of God, beholding God in all, we are empowered to bring Christ to all things: good and evil, happy and suffering, healthy and sick, virtuous and sinful. We bring the mind of Christ to all aspects of our life: to the "good" stuff to affirm it and to the "evil" or "bad" stuff to heal or transform it. The mind of Christ is related to the Greek word *metanoia* which gets translated into English as *repent* but which, if you parse out the Greek, has a meaning closer to *change your mind* or even *go beyond your mind* (*meta: beyond; noia: mind*). In other words, go beyond the dualistic mind, which judges and condemns, into the "beyond normal human" mind of Christ, the consciousness of nonduality, of Divine Love. That is the gate to holiness, the pathway to truly believing the Good News and becoming a force for healing and transformation in a world that so desperately needs it.

*   *   *

To read the Bible *like* a mystic, it helps to learn how to read the Bible *as* a mystic. I understand that most of us are nowhere near the incredible beatitude that we discern when we read the writings of world-class mature mystics like Meister Eckhart, Julian of Norwich, John of the Cross, or Bernadette Roberts. But you don't have to be a genius in order to be a student— and every genius was in kindergarten once. Likewise, to be a mystical seeker makes you, in a very real sense, a mystic— the unique mystic who you are created to be. Read the Bible through *your* eyes, listening to your heart, seeking the guidance of the Spirit who lives in you. Maybe you are just barely on the path of purification or illumination. That's fine; start where you are. Just keep reading and just keep praying, meditating, and contemplating. The deeper you go, the more you will begin to see the treasures that point to a unitive and even nondual experience of God. The mystical life is an exciting adventure; let the Bible—read through eyes that yearn for the love of God—be your companion along the way.

*   *   *

8

Seven Keys to Unlock the Bible

*The mysteries of the faith are not an object for the
intelligence as the faculty which permits affirmation or
denial. They are not of the order of the truth, but above
it. The only part of the human soul capable of real contact with them is the faculty of supernatural love.*

—Simone Weil

*   *   *

Too many people approach the Bible as if it were a textbook
or, worse yet, a code of law. But mystics and contemplatives
have always understood that the Bible is first and foremost
about love, which is why their favorite book in the Bible has
always been the Song of Songs, the juicy love poem at the
heart of the Hebrew wisdom literature. Yes, you can read the
Bible like a textbook (to learn about God) or like a code of law
(to discover and apply God's commandments in our lives),
but both of those approaches to Scripture are meant to be

subordinate to the invitation into love—for, more than any-thing else, God is Love.

The contemplative approach to Scripture means setting aside, even if only for a time, any ideas you might have about *studying* the Bible as a textbook or code of law. To read the Bible in a contemplative or even mystical way means to read Scripture in its entirety as a book of myth, even the parts that are generally accepted as historical. Reading it primarily as a mythological book means to read it primarily for spiritual insight and wisdom and then only secondarily to learn more about what may or may not have happened in the world thousands of years ago. I emphasize *primarily* because there is still an important place for reading the Bible from a historical/critical perspective, although that is primarily the work of scholars, academics, and professional theologians.

If you want to become a writer, you can spend plenty of time learning about grammar, rhetoric, the elements of style, and the rules of composition. Study long enough and hard enough, and you can get to the point where you know the theory of good writing backward and forward. But none of this will get your book or other writing project completed—or make a writer out of you. Sooner or later, you will have to sit down, face the empty page (or screen), and take the plunge of actually recording your thoughts and words. Then you will write and rewrite, edit and revise, but all those steps in the writing process depend on your initial commitment to giving voice to your words.

To read the Bible like a mystic requires a similar commitment. You can read (in addition to this book) the writings and commentaries of so many other teachers, practitioners, theologians, and scholars. But reading about the Bible is not the same thing as simply reading the Bible itself. In this chapter, I offer a list of keys that I believe can help anyone unlock the spiritual treasures of the Bible for themselves. This list includes virtues, values, perspectives, and practices that can help anyone unlock the vault, so to speak, where the treasures of biblical wisdom are stored. Ultimately, of course, your guide to the riches of the Bible must be the Spirit, who guides you in your heart. But I believe these keys are tools you can use to be more available to receive the Spirit's guidance.

To read the Bible like a mystic, here are the keys to keep with you: a spirit of humility, a willingness to love, a commitment to conversation, a desire for wisdom, a hunger for justice, a grounding in prayer, and an openness to Mystery. Let's look at each of these in turn.

Humility

To read the Bible like a mystic, we need to approach the text with humility. Humility is not self-doubt or thinking that you are a worm or anything like that. When I was a child, my mom used to say that someone had an inferiority complex (coming from the language of Adlerian psychoanalysis). Nowadays most of us would say that such a person has dysfunctionally low self-esteem. What's important for our discussion is that this is *not* what is meant by the spiritual virtue of humility. Humility is the open-minded and openhearted recognition that one does not know all the answers or that one's opinion could be inaccurate or incomplete and therefore should be subject to change or revision. Humility is the refreshing and healthy absence of arrogance and smug certainty that one's ideas or views are necessarily right or correct or best.

I remember talking to a friend of mine who attended seminary, and the first course she took was a summer school class on New Testament Greek. But it was more than just learning vocabulary and grammar; it was a crash course in learning how so much of the language of the Bible is ambiguous, subject to multiple interpretations, and prone to being understood in more than one way. As my friend put it, "This course taught me that no one owns the Bible"—in other words, no single person, interpreter, or even church or school of thought can definitively say, "This is the one true absolute meaning of the text." Since no one owns the meaning of the Bible, that means you don't either. Humility is the virtue that recognizes this and is okay with it. It's okay not to have all the answers and not to know all the possible ways a passage could be interpreted. It means to come to the text with an open mind and a childlike heart, willing to learn and sometimes even change one's mind.

*   *   *

Love

Perhaps love should be the first key for mystical Bible reading; after all, love is the first fruit of the Holy Spirit (Galatians 5:22), and the New Testament itself clearly states that God *is* Love (1 John 4:8, 16). But *love* is one of those words that has come to mean so many different things to different people that it has almost become meaningless. Love gets equated with romance, sex, desire, affection, and sentimentality, as well as with charity, compassion, mercy, forgiveness, and kindness. So when we say, "God is Love," which love are we referring to? This is why I decided humility needed to come first: we all need to have basic humility not only regarding our approach to the Bible but also our approach to God. I'm sure I myself don't have anything more than the most rudimentary understanding of what *God is Love* really means, but I take it to understand that when I grow in my sense of love, I am simultaneously growing in my understanding of God. Perhaps even more to the point, when I think about the core principle of God's being as Love, that helps me avoid getting caught up in the idea that God is mostly about wrath, or reward and punishment, or control, or domination, or purity, or any of the countless other ways that we ignore love when we try to understand God. And what goes for God also goes for the Bible. Love is the core message here—not love in any kind of limited human understanding, like the list I just provided, but love in its most transcendental, heavenly, holistic sense: love as ultimate compassion, ultimate concern, ultimate care, ultimate mercy, ultimate kindness, and so forth. To read the Bible through the eyes of mystical love provides a safeguard against getting caught up in seeing the Bible as a textbook for deciding who's good and who's bad or who gets to go to heaven and who doesn't.

When we read the Bible with the eyes of love, we learn that all these dualistic ways of reading it are limited and incomplete and can cause harm—outcomes that the God who is Love definitely does not want. Finally, compassionate love is the best antidote against weaponizing the Bible (using it to prove to ourselves that we are better than "those people"— whoever those people might be).

∗   ∗   ∗

Conversation

There's an old joke that I have heard applied to Jewish rabbis, to Wiccan priestesses, and also to biblical scholars: ask three of them a question, and you'll get five answers. It's not meant to be a criticism of any of those groups of people, although I'm sure some mean-spirited people might interpret it that way. But I see it as a badge of honor, for the joke suggests that part of being a rabbi (or a priestess or a scholar) is being smart enough to understand that sometimes a question can be well answered in more than one way.

I once heard Brian McLaren tell a story about sitting next to a rabbi on a flight. They struck up a conversation, and she said to him, "You know something I don't understand about you Christians? You read the Bible with this attitude that there could only be one 'correct' interpretation of any particular passage. But for us Jews, the Bible is a bottomless well of meaning." I imagine what she meant by that was that Jewish rabbis and scholars actually love how sometimes a verse or passage can be interpreted in multiple ways. This is not a cause for concern but rather a cause for conversation—for we need to rely on each other, and learn from one another, in order to discern what might be the best or wisest interpretation of a passage, at least in any one particular time or place. One of the reasons I love this idea of the bottomless well of meaning is that it suggests the Bible might have a different message for different people, depending on our circumstances.

To bring a spirit of conversation to your reading of the Bible means you are bringing a willingness to live with this tension, recognizing how different people might see different meanings in the same passage. To read the Bible like a mystic means we can welcome this tension and learn from it, but we don't have to try to eliminate it or "fix" it or manage it.

Meanwhile, there's another sense in which we need to bring conversation to our encounter with the Bible: the way we read the Bible needs to be in conversation with other ways of knowing or understanding or making sense of the world. So we need to let the knowledge of science be in conversation with the Bible, and the wisdom of other faith traditions be in conversation with the Bible, and even the wisdom of different political beliefs or philosophies or psychology and sociology and so forth. And we need to be in conversation with people who are different from us. Whites need to read the Bible in conversation with people of color, men need to read the Bible in conversation with women, cisgender people need to read the Bible in conversation with transgender and nonbinary people, able-bodied people need to read the Bible with people with disabilities, straight folks need to read the Bible in conversation with queer folks, wealthy or educated folks need to be in conversation with poor or uneducated people, and the list could go on.

* * *

Wisdom

We saw in chapter 7 how Origen of Alexandria used three wisdom writings in the Bible—Proverbs, Ecclesiastes, and the Song of Songs—to develop his model for the mystical life encompassing purification, illumination, and union. Those three books are part of an entire section of the writings in the Hebrew Scriptures known as *wisdom literature*; this includes Job, Psalms, Proverbs, Ecclesiastes, and the Song of Songs (Catholic and Orthodox Bibles include a few other books of wisdom literature). The wisdom books are distinctive because they tend to be poetic with a practical or down-to-earth focus on what is helpful or necessary for living a good and happy life; unlike the "law" books that tend to focus on commandments, regulations, and purity codes, the wisdom literature tends to be more philosophical and open-ended. In other words, wisdom is less about cut-and-dried rules to follow and instead highlights a more thoughtful and discerning approach to the messages being offered.

What exactly is wisdom? Helpfully, Proverbs offers a useful definition: "For God gives wisdom; from God's mouth comes knowledge and understanding" (Proverbs 2:6). In other words, wisdom is more than just an accumulation of facts and figures or rules and regulations (knowledge); it also involves understanding—in other words, a thoughtful and flexible capacity to apply knowledge in helpful or appropriate ways. In the Rule of Saint Benedict (the guide for monasteries written some 1,500 years ago), the author points out that different monks need to be treated in different ways, depending on their maturity, intelligence, personality, and so forth. All monks must follow the same common set of rules, but the abbot (leader) of the monastery must use discernment in how the rules are applied to the circumstances surrounding each individual monk. This is why society depends on judges, counselors, ministers, and others whose job it is to use thoughtful understanding to apply universal standards or principles in specific ways, depending on the circumstances at hand.

Bringing the quality of wisdom to how we read the Bible means we need to resist the temptation to see Scripture as a kind of cut-and-dried technical manual or, worse, as a legal code book (yes, there are sections of the Bible that were, in fact, historical legal codes, but they are only a small percentage of the entire book, and much of their content was radically reinterpreted by both the prophets and then Jesus himself). Instead of seeing the Bible as a technical manual, wisdom requires us to see it as a rich and multivoiced source book for learning how to respond to the love and guidance of God in our lives—in other words, the entire book (even the "legal" bits) is primarily about growing in wisdom, which means both knowledge and understanding/discernment.

* * *

Justice

Ever since the snake suggested to Eve and Adam that there was more to living in the garden of Eden than just following the rules, conflict has been a part of the stories of the Bible. Any writer will point out that you can't have a good story without conflict—and the Bible is more than just a good story; it's also a record of how human beings try to relate to God. Meanwhile, the Bible is also bluntly realistic about the fact that conflict exists not only between humans and God but also among humans themselves—and pretty early on, it becomes obvious that God stands for justice, even though many human beings seem to be entirely committed to promoting their own self-interest, no matter how unjust or harmful such actions might be. Early in the book of the prophet Isaiah, we see this principle clearly spelled out: "Learn to do good; seek justice, rescue the oppressed, defend the orphan, plead for the widow" (Isaiah 1:17). Seeking justice and goodness is paired with fighting against oppression and supporting the most vulnerable members of society, including those whose family situations have left them without the resources they need to thrive.

It seems pretty obvious, especially when reading the prophets but also Jesus (see Matthew 25), that God has a preference for the underdog, those who are vulnerable, oppressed, or victimized. Unfortunately, we human beings are not always as conscious of social inequality or systems of power and privilege. For this reason, I believe paying close attention to justice is necessary for a truly contemplative approach to the Bible. When pondering the meaning of a passage, be sure to consider how the wisdom you are encountering can make a difference to those who suffer under life's injustices. No one person can single-handedly fight all the unfairness in the world, but we all do have a responsibility not to *add* to injustice, which means we need to read the Bible with God's commitment to justice clearly in mind.

* * *

Prayer

"Pray without ceasing" is one of the most concise words of instruction offered in the Bible (from the apostle Paul in 1 Thessalonians 5:17). Jesus's students and followers pressed him for guidance about how to pray well. Clearly, prayer is at the heart of faith, even if many people (and, sadly, even many churches) don't make prayer a priority. Spiritual people who don't bother to pray are like athletes who don't work out. Sooner or later, you'll lose your edge.

Think of it this way: professors teach; lawyers litigate; doctors heal; artists create art. In a similar way, mystics and contemplatives *pray*. That's what makes them who they are. Now, prayer is like so many other spiritual topics, something that is easily misunderstood; many people associate prayer with words they memorized as a child: "Now I lay me down to sleep" or "God is great, God is good." All it takes is going to school and facing a text or exam for which you don't feel adequately prepared, and even the most seasoned agnostic might find themselves offering up a prayer "just in case." But prayer is more than just reciting a formulaic incantation or asking God for favors (as if God were our celestial butler). For mystics and contemplatives, prayer is anything we do to respond to Divine Love in our lives. Yes, this can include offering verbal words of adoration, thanksgiving, confession, or petition, but the mystical tradition is clear that prayer ultimately shades off into meditation, contemplation, and even pure silence, where the emphasis is not on a kind of transactional exchange but rather time, energy, and attention invested into fostering a deepening relationship with the Mystery we call *God.*

So to read the Bible like a mystic, perhaps more than anything else what we really need to do is *pray* the Bible like a mystic. Approach your time with the sacred text not as an exercise in learning about God (although it certainly can be that) but rather as an opportunity to meet the Spirit directly—not so much just in the ancient words on the page but in your own heart and mind as you encounter those words. In other words, reading the Bible is a way to hang out with God, to spend time consciously seeking a deeper sense of the divine presence in your heart. There's so much I could say about what this could look like, but here I'd just like to point out one important detail: if we are going to pray the Bible, then we need to learn to be honest in our prayer. If we read something in the Bible that confuses us, pray about being confused. If we read something that makes us angry or upset, or we find ourselves feeling uncomfortable in response to something we've read, it's helpful to simply bring all those feelings to the Mystery we call God. There is no need to try to impress God; the Spirit is not like some visiting regional manager or auditors for whom we must put our best foot forward. On the contrary, God is more like a caring doctor who can only help us reach our maximum level of health and wellness to the extent that we are completely honest.

*   *   *

Mystery

The final principle to bring to your reading of the Bible is one of my favorite words for describing God: *Mystery*. By mystery, I don't mean an enigma to be solved in a kind of Nancy Drew sense but rather a deeper Mystery (with a capital M) that is beyond any human capacity to figure out. I suppose I could have just said that the seventh principle to bring to the Bible is God's own presence in our hearts, but I know that many people read the Bible because they *don't* feel God's presence, or they're not really even sure God exists at all.

No matter what your understanding or experience of God might be, I believe that *Mystery* is something that shows up in every human life. We all know that life is strange and mysterious, filled with profound pleasures but also great suffering. We all want love, yet many of us struggle with loneliness or deeply dissatisfying relationships. We all want abundance, but many of us live in poverty or financial insecurity or have lives that have become spiritually impoverished through stress, addiction, or conflict. If we live long enough, we will eventually experience the decline that comes with aging and the challenges of illness, frailty, and perhaps cognitive impairment. No matter what else or which circumstances meet us in the meantime, we all know we are going to die someday. Whether that is next week or decades from now, when it arrives, it will probably feel like it is coming too soon.

But life has so many wonders as well: the beauty of nature, the thrill of romance, the joy of sports, the mind-expanding pleasure we take in creativity or meditation or entertainment. Most living creatures struggle hard when it seems that injury or death is near, which says that even at a deep and perhaps unconscious level, most of us know that this mysterious life is worth living.

Mystery shares the first syllable of *mysticism* for a reason. Both words are related to a Greek root word that evokes a sense of silence and hiddenness (the word *mute*, like the mute button on your phone or Zoom, also comes from that same source). So in bringing a sense of Mystery to Scripture, I'm suggesting that you look for silence, wonder, unknowing, insight, imagination, reverie, and curiosity when you sit down to read. Mystery is, I believe, related to humility since they both imply that we come to the text with an open and almost childlike recognition that we don't have all the answers. But whereas humility is simply that openness, Mystery is an invitation to step directly into the unknowing, into the silence, trusting that wisdom and love and insight and understanding will meet us even in the darkness, the silence, and the unknowing (which means it might be working on us at a level below our conscious awareness). To read the Bible with a sense of Mystery means allowing the text to take you to the place of wonder and willingness and then to let all the other principles we have discussed—love, discernment, wisdom, prayer, and so forth—shape our experience of the words we read. Reading the Bible like a mystic means accepting when you don't have it all figured out and learning to trust that the Mystery is more than just an unsolvable puzzle: it is a name for the very One you are seeking. Encounter the text with a listening heart and a wondering mind and then see where it takes you.

9

Scripture and Spiritual Transformation

To think of oneself as a child of God is a liberating experience—it is to free oneself from all feelings of inferiority—whether of race, or color, or sex, or age, or economic status, or position in life. When I say that I am a child of God—made in his image—(the theologians like to use the term imago dei*)—I imply that "Black is beautiful," that White is beautiful, that Red is beautiful, or Yellow is beautiful. I do not need to make special pleading for my sex—male or female or in-between—to bolster self-esteem. When I truly believe that God is my Father and Mother, in short, my Creator, I am bound also to believe that all men, women, and children of whatever race, color, creed, or ethnic origin are my sisters- and brothers-in-Christ—whether they are Anglicans, Roman Catholics, Methodists, Black Muslims, members of the Judaic faith, Russian Orthodox, Buddhists, or atheists.*

—Pauli Murray

WHEN I USED to work for the Trappist monks, one time I was given the task to sort through some old books in the library to see if any were worth preserving or if they should be donated to create room for new acquisitions. As I was going through the books, I discovered a musty old tome with the title *A Spiritual Directory for Religious*, written by a European monk named Vitalis Lehodey. I asked Father Tom Francis, one of the elderly monks, what it was. "Oh, that was an important book when I was a novice," he reminisced. "It was basically a guidebook for how to grow spiritually as a monk." I asked him if it was a book I should read, given my own hunger for spiritual growth. Fr. Tom pointed out that it was originally written in French over a hundred years ago, that it was very old-school and really only intended for monks. So I never read it; still, this idea of a book designed to guide us in our spiritual growth stayed with me—until I realized one day that's really what the Bible is (or what it's meant to be): a "directory" or book designed to direct us on our journey of spiritual growth and transformation.

Okay, then, how can the Bible be our "spiritual directory"—whether we think of ourselves as mystics, or contemplatives, or simply humble seekers? How can a person in our time read the Bible specifically for the purpose of spiritual growth? As I prayed and reflected on this concept, I was inspired to draw up this list of seven intentions or mindsets that I believe are most conducive to reading the Bible from a mystical or spiritual growth-seeking perspective. I invite you to reflect on each of these intentions, see which ones naturally resonate with you, and consider how you can incorporate all of these mindsets into your own journey with Scripture.

* * *

Read the Bible to Be Transformed into a More Creative and Compassionate Person

The poet William Blake once said, "The man who never alters his opinion is like standing water, and breeds reptiles of the mind" (this is true for people of all genders). One of the easiest ways to grow old before your time is to cement your mind, values, and beliefs into just one way of seeing things. When we say someone is "set in their ways," it is rarely meant as a compliment.

So to read the Bible like a mystic, read it with the same kind of expectancy you would bring to a date with a new friend (or romantic interest)—a mind and heart opened to new possibilities and new ways of seeing things. When we begin to work with a teacher or mentor, we do it with a clear understanding that this new person in our lives will challenge us to see things in a new way. With that in mind, allow the Bible to be your literary mentor: a collection of voices from the distant past whose words, wisdom, and mistakes can bring you to a place of inner change, growth, and transformation.

When we first start to work with a mentor, life coach, or spiritual director, the person will often ask us, "Why are you here?" Why do you want the guidance or inspiration that comes from someone who can teach or guide you? (I should point out here that many spiritual directors view not themselves but the indwelling Spirit as your true director or guide.) Just as it's important to know what you want from a coach or a mentor, knowing what you want from the Bible will give you a richer and deeper experience of reading it. From the perspective of the mystics, there is one overriding reason to dive into the Bible: to draw closer to God. But what does that mean? I'd like to suggest that since God is Love (I John 4:8, 16), and God is the Creator (Genesis 1:1), and furthermore that human beings are created in God's image and likeness (Genesis 1:27), then the ultimate purpose for reading the Bible, at least mystically speaking, is not only to know God better but also to seek God's transforming presence in our hearts, a presence that is made known to us by how we slowly but gradually become more loving/compassionate and creative in our lives.

Of course, the Bible is not a how-to manual on becoming more creative or compassionate; that ultimately is a direct gift from the Spirit in our hearts. But creativity and caring are recurring themes in Scripture, so a truly contemplative engagement with the text will give us inspiration and insight to help us grow (with the Spirit's grace) in those ways.

* * *

Read the Bible to Become More Committed to Justice and the Dismantling of Systemic Privilege

Transformation doesn't just happen to us as lone individuals. One of the first teachings of the Bible, found early in the book of Genesis, is the principle that human beings are meant to be in relationship with one another; God is recorded as saying, "It is not good for a human being to be alone" (indeed, this is the first instance in the Bible where something is labeled as "not good," implying that it is a situation that needs change, transformation, or healing). We are not meant to be all alone; indeed, we know that people who live in sustained periods of solitude can experience tremendous psychological stress. So if community is such an important part of being human, it only stands to reason that the kind of spiritual transformation we seek through reading a sacred book like the Bible would not just be a matter of personal, individual self-improvement but would have a social or communal dimension to it as well.

We've seen how traditional religious language speaks about personal transformation in terms of *sin* and *repentance*. Sin is any thought, word, or deed that serves to alienate us from love for God or neighbor. In the English language, *sin* has come to carry a connotation of moral failing or outright rejection of God, but the original sense of the word was subtler: it simply meant *missing the mark* like a poorly aimed arrow flies wide of its target. In our day, we have become conscious of the fact that some of the ways we shut down to love may have nothing to do with arrogantly rejecting it; instead, many of our unloving behaviors can be traced back to addiction, mental illness, or psychological trauma that has left us wounded and defensive. This is why I prefer to avoid the sin talk and focus instead on how we are wounded and need healing from the God who is infinite Love.

The language of sin doesn't often get applied to how our communities or societies can also turn away from love on a collective level. We are more likely to see collective sin in terms of injustice, oppression, or systems of privilege and power. But just like individual "sin," these collective wounds are often the result of complex dynamics of intergenerational trauma and cultural conditions that work to benefit some people at the expense of others. I point this out because I often see an unfortunate tendency among Christians (and others) to get caught up in blame whenever we talk about situations like personal sin or systemic injustice.

If you want to reflect on who is to blame because problems like racism, sexism, homophobia, transphobia, and entrenched economic inequality exist, I encourage you to read some of the great writings by philosophers, sociologists, economists, psychologists, politicians, and others who have studied such problems and are working hard to dismantle the inequities in the world today. That kind of structural analysis is a little outside of what the Bible has to offer.

What *does* the Bible have to offer? Remember, it is a book of myths and stories; a recurring theme is that God tends to favor anyone who suffers because of social inequities or oppression. God is a God of justice and fairness. This message is found throughout the prophets of the Hebrew Scriptures and is echoed by Jesus in the New Testament.

So a mystical reading of the Bible does not limit itself to questions of "how can I, personally, be transformed by the wisdom in this sacred book?" The larger questions that would go along with that are: How can the wisdom of this book help not only individuals to be transformed but also society as a whole? And what can I do to play my part in helping to make the world a better place?

* * *

Read the Bible to Absorb Its Distinctive Wisdom While Integrating It within the Perennial Tradition

This principle will likely be controversial among some old-school Christians, let alone those who espouse authoritarian or fundamentalist beliefs. Well, so be it. I think we have to be clear about what a mystical approach to the Bible invites us into.

In the past, many Christians regarded the Bible as the "one true sacred text"—in other words, the only possible book, out of the millions of writings found around the world and throughout history, to be the expression of God's own word. Indeed, one of the nicknames for the Bible is *the word of God*. There's a long-standing principle within Christianity that the Bible contains all things necessary for salvation. The idea is very simple: if you want to go to heaven after you die (that's how many Christians understand salvation), then you must read the Bible, obey its teachings, and ignore any other book, sacred or otherwise, that contradicts it.

Let's call a fig a fig: this kind of thinking is religious chauvinism at its worst. It is based on a limited image of God and simply fails to address the reality of life in a world filled with religious and spiritual diversity.

The Bible contains many different voices, and at times they clearly contradict one another. Given that the Bible can't even get its own act together, why should we be prohibited from reading and considering the wisdom of other books that may offer a different perspective?

The limited way of thinking about the Bible reduces God to some sort of capricious bully, a miser who is only willing to give all of humanity just one sacred book and then goes on to punish anyone who finds meaning and purpose and inspiration in any other philosophy. That's not a God of Love—that's a sadistic abuser. I believe any thinking human being is not only justified in rejecting such an amoral "god" but is in fact ethically obligated to do so.

Many mystics in the Christian tradition, especially in the present day but also throughout history, have paired their devotion to Christianity with a willingness to study and/or be in dialogue with the wisdom of other faiths. This goes all the way back to the second century, when one of Christianity's earliest mystics, Clement of Alexandria, wrote about Christianity in the light of pagan Greek philosophy and spirituality. He was the first of a long line, including Ramon Lull, a medieval philosopher who wrote positively about Judaism and Islam; Evelyn Underhill, the English mystic who used Jewish, Sufi, and Eastern writings to illustrate her own mystical work; and a wide array of twentieth-century figures who explored the essential unity between Christianity and other faiths, such as Thomas Merton, Bede Griffiths, Howard Thurman, Tilden Edwards, Ruben Habito, Paul Knitter, Sara Grant, Abhishiktananda, Elaine MacInnes, Hugo Enomiya-Lassalle, and many others.

Sadly, Christians who positively explore or interact with other faiths and spiritual traditions have always been in the minority, and there are plenty of Christian theologians, ministers, and ordinary laypeople who are convinced it would be a horrible sin to "cheat" on God by exploring other faiths. But the whole point behind this book is to explore a *mystical* approach to the Bible, and for the most part, the Christians who do engage in positive engagement with other faiths and wisdom traditions have tended to be the contemplatives and the mystics.

To read the Bible like a mystic, read it like a good citizen of Planet Earth. Look at the wisdom of the Bible in the light of all the great wisdom traditions on our beautiful planet; don't expect the Bible to give you unshakable "answers" that cannot be questioned or engaged with critically. On the contrary, be willing to balance the wisdom you find in this sacred text with wisdom that comes from other sources, including (but not limited to) Judaism, Islam, Hinduism, Buddhism, and Indigenous spiritualities from around the world. The Bible can be seen as contributing to a variety of voices of wisdom and insight, creating harmony (and, on occasion, disharmony) with those we can meet through sacred texts.

Philosophers from the Renaissance to the present speak of the *perennial philosophy* to suggest there is a golden thread of wisdom that belongs to all of humanity, and each sacred tradition or religion offers a beautiful, but limited, understanding of this universal wisdom. Perennialism is not anti-Christian—but it does indeed reject any idea that only one path can be the "one true" path. Christians who are dedicated to rejecting all other faiths beyond their own are not likely to find a warm welcome among perennialists, but those who are mystically inclined will find that their thirst for wisdom can be quenched through many wells.

You do not have to be a perennialist to be a contemplative or a mystic. Diving exclusively into Christian mysticism can be a richly rewarding and entirely satisfying spiritual practice; I know plenty of contemplative Christians who do not explore other faiths, and that's certainly fine. But they recognize there is good to be found in all traditions, so they don't reject other faiths as erroneous or evil.

When you read the Bible to seek the wisdom within it, weigh its teachings with insights that come from other traditions. If you feel called to walk the Christian path exclusively, follow your heart—but when you read the Bible, remember you are reading one (but not the only) classic of literature that documents the age-old adventure of humanity seeking deeper intimacy with the divine.

* * *

Read the Bible to Foster Creative Dialogue among Spirituality, Science, and Philosophy

Reading Scripture with appreciation for the wisdom of all the world's religious, spiritual, and mystical traditions is just the beginning. Most people are familiar with the story of Galileo, the Renaissance astronomer who used a telescope to discover, among other things, that Jupiter was a planet with moons orbiting it, which led to his advocacy for the idea that the sun, not the Earth, was the center of the solar system. Because Catholic teaching at that time held to a geocentric (as opposed to heliocentric) understanding of the cosmos, he was accused of heresy and forced to recant (publicly disavow his scientific opinions). It was not until the late twentieth century that the Catholic Church as an institution finally admitted that Galileo was right (talk about slow on the uptake).

The moral of Galileo's story is simple: whatever you may think of the Bible's value as a book of spiritual wisdom, it's not much help when it comes to empirical science. And so the next principle for reading the Bible like a mystic is to accept that it should be read in a humble way, especially in relation to other forms of human knowledge, specifically science, philosophy, psychology, and sociology.

Once we accept that the "science" of the Bible is limited by the time in which it was written—and that human knowledge has continued to expand in the centuries and millennia since—we are liberated from having to squeeze all of human knowledge into a Bible-shaped container. Instead, we can regard the Bible as an important document in the overall history of human knowledge and intelligence, acknowledging its limitations but also reading it in an honest and balanced way. No, the Bible can't tell you much about astronomy, geology, ancient history, or other hard sciences—nor does it really understand human sexuality, gender diversity, addiction, trauma, and recovery. But as a collection of mythic stories and insightful wisdom, it still has much to offer the human family. If we insist that the Bible should be all things to all people, we not only are intellectually dishonest, but we also end up trying to make the Bible itself something it's not—and this plays into the hands of atheists and other cynics who reject even the spiritual wisdom in the Bible because of the way that fundamentalist Christians have tried to make it the only reliable source of not only wisdom but knowledge as well.

So read the Bible with the same mind of a scientist who is weighing evidence. If something seems off, explore it, do more research, and look for the most accurate, balanced, and honest theory to understand what's going on. People who insist on reading the Bible with blinders on so that they reject the rest of human knowledge are being neither honest nor accurate; they are willfully ignoring human knowledge in order to remain addicted to their narrow interpretation of the Bible. Mystics, who are not afraid of knowledge, rightly reject such limited ways of thinking.

* * *

Read the Bible to Deepen Your Ability to Integrate Mythic Wisdom into Your Own Spiritual Path

If the Bible is not the only true or inerrant word of God, and if it cannot be seen as a substitute for science or other branches of human knowledge, then why should we read it? Again, the mystics show us the way. To read the Bible like a mystic, we accept it for what it is—a book that includes some ancient history but mostly is a treasury of mythology and stories recounting how generations of Hebrews, Jews, and early Christians sought to make sense of God in their lives. Our next principle for how to read the Bible is to lean into it as a mythical work of art. We read mythic spirituality for one reason: to get inspiration for our own spiritual journey (both individually and collectively). We dug into this principle in some detail in chapter 5.

The English mystic Caryll Houselander speaks to how this way of approaching the Bible works. In her classic book *The Reed of God*, she points out how different aspects of the story of Jesus can be related to any person's spiritual life:

* * *

> *In some He is newly born.*
> *In some He is a child.*
> *In some He is homeless.*
> *In some He is ignored, unrecognised, mocked,*
> *betrayed.*
> *In some He is hungry; in some He is naked; in some*
> *He is helpless.*
> *Here are examples, but they are not exhaustive:*
> *indeed, they are only hints at the countless*
> *manifestations of Christ in man.*

The story of Jesus is much more than just some historical document about a person who lived two thousand years ago. As a work of mythic imagination, it invites us to find the Christ who lives in our hearts right here and now. When we are suffering, we are Christ crucified. When we are happy, we are Christ transfigured. When we have started something new, we are Christ resurrected. The more familiar you are with the stories of Jesus in the New Testament, the more examples you can think of this.

A mystical reader does not just study Jesus to learn facts and figures about something that happened two thousand years ago but reads the stories to find meaning and insight into what is happening in their life today and how they can find Christ and/or the Holy Spirit in their life and heart—right here and now.

*   *   *

Read the Bible to Foster Your Mystical Imagination as a Doorway to Meditation and Contemplation

Great saints and mystics like Aelred of Rievaulx and Ignatius of Loyola—as well as spiritual guides of our own time, like James Martin or Margaret Silf—have long recognized that the imagination is a powerful doorway into prayer (we looked at this in chapter 5). Jesus taught us to love God with our "whole mind" (among other ways of loving God), and part of the wholeness of the mind is the capacity to imagine. So when we use our imagination in the service of drawing closer to God, we can trust that God will bless our longing for God and grace us with the capacity to know God better through our inner experience. This isn't foolproof, of course: the capacity for self-delusion is, unfortunately, a part of spiritual practice as much as any other area of life, but by discerning our experiences in the light of spiritual direction or by consulting the wisdom of the mystics, it is reasonable to trust that our imaginal encounter with the God of Love can be a profound way to grow closer to that God.

What works for prayer also works for reading the Bible. Whenever you read the Bible, you can use your imagination to visualize that you are actually present in the story you are reading about and that Christ and/or the Holy Spirit is present with you now, reading along with you and available to imaginatively interpret the text you are reading.

*   *   *

Read the Bible to Encounter, Know, and Deepen Intimacy with the Spirit Who Resides Within

I hope you can see how all the previous intentions really led up to this one. This is the heart of reading the Bible like a mystic. Yes, read it like a scholar: be sure to ask all the hard questions. Read it like a true believer: trust that God can speak to you through it. Even read it like an agnostic and be willing to notice whenever your intuition recoils from a passage because it appears sexist, or homophobic, or presents God as violent or capricious. Reading the Bible in a mystical way does not negate any of these other approaches, but it takes us further: it consents to being an ongoing part of this great story of how humanity, over the centuries, has responded to the love of God. You, today, read the Bible as part of *your* response to Divine Love, *your* consent to the Spirit's presence and action in your life. As you explore the Bible, you will be struck by its beauty, inspired

by its insight, frustrated by its emphasis on laws and regulations, and horrified by its cultural obsolescence. Whatever your
response may be, it is an opportunity to be more authentic,
more honest, more present to the God who lives in your heart
as absolute and unconditional Love (with a capital L). Read
the Bible to seek to know Divine Love and to know the Divine
Lover better. Is there any other reason, ultimately, to read it? All
the other purposes or intentions for reading the Bible (to learn,
grow, be challenged, be inspired, etc.) all boil down to this one
ultimate reason. Read the Bible to let Love love you—through
it and through the totality of your life.

*   *   *

Applying These Keys to Your Own Encounter with the Bible

These seven transformational intentions are intended to support your own journey into the mystical life. Remember the
three phases or stages of purification, illumination, and union.
We seek to release anything in our lives that interferes with
our desire to grow intimate with God; that's purification.
Then we seek to simply appreciate what it means to be in
an ever-deepening relationship with the Divine; that's illumination. Finally, we acknowledge that through no effort or
achievement of our own, the grace of the spiritual life invites us
to recognize something that has been real all along: that God's

Spirit has been poured into our hearts, and we are indeed one with that Spirit. When you ponder these seven purposes for reading the Bible like a mystic, the first two are the keys to reading it for purification; the next two are keys for reading the Bible for illumination, and the final three are the keys for reading it to realize and recognize our graced union with the Divine. Put another way, keys 1 and 2 invite us into *goodness*; keys 3 and 4 invite us into *truth*; and keys 5, 6, and 7 invite us into *beauty*. Learning to find what is good, what is true, and what is beautiful in the Bible (and in our own hearts) is also an important part of the mystical life.

*   *   *

To all of this I would add one more overriding principle: Don't go it alone. Seek to read the Bible in a communal way. This could involve working with a spiritual director with whom you can bounce around your questions, concerns, or befuddlements when encountering Scripture or participating in a prayer circle or even a Bible study group, as long as there is an understanding that the Bible can be read not just for scholarly knowledge but also for spiritual growth. If all else fails, get to know some of the amazing resources and commentaries that are available to help you read the Bible from a spiritual or contemplative perspective. As an ancient and complex work of spiritual literature, the Bible is not always an easy book to read, so getting guidance from others who share your hunger for spiritual growth can be enormously helpful.

❧ 10 ❧

Read the Bible like a Mystic

Wise people know their wisdom is not self-generated. It comes from a larger and deeper Source, which is always shared (some psychologists call this the collective unconscious and Christians call it the Holy Spirit).

—Richard Rohr

*   *   *

MYSTICS—AT LEAST CHRISTIAN mystics—love to read the Bible. They've been reading it ever since it was written, and it's reasonable to assume the biblical writers were mystics as well, which means the Bible has been a part of Western mysticism since before the ink got dry when the words were first committed to paper. In every succeeding generation, the writings of the mystics reveal that they were steeped in the words and wisdom of Scripture. They quote Scripture all the time, often without even providing chapter and verse citation. The expectation was that anyone who would read the writings of the mystics was probably as deeply immersed in Scripture as the mystics themselves. For centuries, most of the great mystics were monks, nuns, or priests, which means their lives were structured around daily prayer and regular exposure to the Bible through the shared prayer (liturgy) of their community. Today, very few of us live in monasteries or even visit them, so we are at a disadvantage when it comes to the Bible. On the other hand, in ancient times when Bibles had to be copied by hand, very few people could afford to own one which means we are immeasurably blessed—thanks to smart phones and the internet, most people in our society have immediate access to the Bible wherever they go.

* * *

Mystics quote Scripture the way you and I might make references to whatever is currently trending on social media. The Bible provided mystics of old with the cultural language and imaginative imagery by which they structured their spiritual lives and patterns of communication. Some of that still lives in the idioms and proverbs we find in our language: *the patience of Job, turn the other cheek, forbidden fruit, the writing on the wall, the twinkling of an eye, faith that can move mountains—* these are just a few biblical phrases and images that remain part of our common tongue. But compared to how deeply the imaginations of ancient mystics were shaped by the biblical text, we children of the third millennium have a lot to learn.

* * *

For mystics, reading the Bible is not an academic exercise nor necessarily a way of making an argument or contributing to a debate (although certainly the Bible has long been used for promoting this or that point of view). Rather, for a mystic, reading the Bible is like meditating or praying or doing yoga. It is simply a daily practice for spiritual care. Contemplation is a way of praying without words, so reading the Bible is a natural companion practice: an ideal way to pray *with* words— ancient words that we have inherited from generations before us, all committed to finding in these words (the words of the Bible) ways to draw closer to God.

*   *   *

When we talk about reading the Bible like a mystic, we are not talking about Bible study, the academic approach to Scripture. This is not meant to imply that biblical scholarship is unnecessary or useless—on the contrary. Prayer may be the best way to access the inner wisdom of the Scriptures, but prayer without study is blind. So this is not either/or; it's both/and. The Bible is an ancient text written in languages and in a culture that, for most of us today, are strange and alien. We need careful scholarship and learned commentary to navigate our way through the sacred text. If you want to read the Bible like a mystic, your primary task is to pray the Bible, but you still need to cultivate a thoughtful, intelligent, and academically sound understanding of it as well. If you want to get physically fit, you must exercise, but you also must eat good food.

Reading the Bible like a mystic is learning how to "work out" with the Bible in a prayerful way, but it still requires "eating the good food" of sound biblical study.

*   *   *

There is no "one-size-fits-all" in the world of the mystics. So part of learning how to read the Bible like a mystic is learning enough about the different mystics to find which mystical approach sings to you.

*   *   *

To be a mystic means to seek the hidden things of God, to embody the hidden presence of God, and to live the unitive life given to us by God. An ongoing question among spiritual seekers is: Are mystics unusual and therefore somewhat special, or is the mystical life meant for everybody? We know that some mystics are renowned for their extraordinary encounters with God—their stories are filled with remarkable visions, miracles, heightened states of consciousness, ecstasies, raptures, and illuminations or enlightenment. They are truly the heroes of the spiritual life, larger-than-life figures who blow us away with the depth and insight of their wisdom. But not all mystics are so amazing and incredible. Others are known for their humility, their simplicity and ordinariness, their down-to-earth qualities and characteristics. Julian of Norwich, Meister Eckhart, and Teresa of Ávila are examples of extraordinary mystics, while Thérèse of Lisieux, Pauli Murray, and Evelyn

Underhill are examples of down-to-earth mystics. Some others, like Howard Thurman or Caryll Houselander, seem to fall in between the humble and the marvelous: these mystics have some remarkable stories to tell, but for the most part, their spirituality still seems to be beautifully ordinary. The moral of the story is that mystics come in all shapes and sizes.

*   *   *

I belong to the "mysticism is for everyone" camp. I don't believe God is in the business of separating us out into elites and plebeians. Yes, like with musical ability or athletic prowess, some people are innately more gifted than others; it's pretty obvious that some people have a more natural aptitude toward spiritual consciousness than others. But everyone has some sort of spiritual capacity for seeking the hidden things of God, embodying the hidden presence of God, and manifesting the unitive life that is always a gift given to us by God.

*   *   *

But to the extent that we try to fulfill that mystical capacity in our lives, how does this impact the way we read the Bible?

*   *   *

A person dedicated to a mystical way of life will read the Bible primarily for the purpose of discovering the hidden things of God insofar as they are hidden in the sacred text. By discovering the hidden mysteries embedded in Scripture, mystics more readily recognize those same mysteries as they emerge within their own lives, their own environments, their own relationships, even their own bodies. It is not controversial to say that God is hidden in the Bible, for the Bible itself says that God is a God who hides (see Isaiah 45:15) and that God is present everywhere (Psalm 139:7–12). Holding both of these ideas as equally true, we can say it makes sense to read the Bible to find the presence of God, although often we experience that divine presence as a hidden (*mystical*) presence, and perhaps all we consciously feel is the mystery of God's seeming absence.

*   *   *

The mystical life is a matter of playing hide-and-seek with our loving, playful God, who seeks to seduce us into responding to Divine Love by beguiling us into seeking God wherever God is hidden. So mystics read the Bible because it is a wonderful text for playing this game of mystical hide-and-seek.

*   *   *

Sometimes the Bible reveals God immediately, as in such beautiful passages as the Sermon on the Mount (Matthew 5–7) or the love chapter (1 Corinthians 13) or the supreme love poem of the Bible, the Song of Songs. Other times, the Bible seems to make God's hidden presence even more fully obscure, as in passages that focus on the harsh language of God's "anger" or the seemingly obsessive details of the purity codes found in the third book of the Bible, Leviticus. So mystics read the

Bible to find God, knowing that at some times this is easier to do than others.

* * *

The Bible is not just a book about God; it is also a book about humanity—about the experience of being human. In that sense, the Bible is a profoundly honest book, for it shows the human experience, warts and all. It's harder to find God in the Bible when Scripture records the shadow sides of human aggression and dysfunction, from our propensity to violence to the fearmongering of xenophobia or the codified oppression of sexism or rigid gender boundaries. There are times when the Bible appears to condone slavery, or mandate violence against foreigners and practitioners of other religions, or approve of genocide. In these ways, the Bible almost completely succeeds in making God so hidden that most readers would simply miss the divine presence, so appalling are the terrible things being written about.

* * *

The mystics remind us, however, that the Bible reveals God to us also by revealing all that is *not* God, and so we must be careful not to confuse the false flags of the Bible that make it seem like God stands for violence or sexism or oppression, when in fact the overall message of the Bible makes it clear that God is opposed to all those things.

*   *   *

Ultimately, though, mystics read the Bible not just to find God in it but also to find God in themselves and in each other. Jesus said, "I am the light of the world" and also that *"you* are the light of the world" (*you* refers to anyone in any time and place—anyone who has ever heard or read those words). He also said, "The kingdom of heaven is among you" and "the kingdom of heaven is within you" (in Greek, this is the same sentence, for the Greek word *entos* can be translated as either *within* or *among*). Hold these words of Jesus together, and the implication is breathtaking: we are all filled with the presence of the divine, and our job is to simultaneously find that divine presence in our own hearts and in each other's hearts. Spoiler alert: that's easier with people we like, more challenging—but no less necessary—with people who trigger us or push our buttons.

*   *   *

The Bible is a cultural treasure, a gift not only to Jews and Christians but also to people of all spiritual paths. It invites us into the mystical life because it gives us a detailed cultural "treasure map" to help us find God—within ourselves and within each other. To read the Bible like a mystic is not to deny the importance of good scholarship, or of seeking guidance for moral and ethical wisdom, or even of questioning those sections of the Bible that seem obsolete or outdated. What ultimately limits the authoritarian, the academic, and the atheist approaches to the Bible is that they are, in themselves, too narrow. The fundamentalist needs the skepticism of the atheist, and the scholar needs the faith of the true believer. The contemplative approach weaves together the faith of the believer, the doubt of the agnostic, and the perseverance of the scholar to create a foundation for a *prayerful* way of encountering the words in Scripture.

*   *   *

If you aren't familiar with *lectio divina* or Ignatian prayer, the two best-known methods for contemplative engagement with the Bible, read on to the appendix. But to read the Bible like a mystic takes us one step further, beyond even the contemplative approach. Reading the Bible like a mystic means engaging the spiritual imagination to trust, radically, that God is present in all things—including the Bible itself—and that the hidden presence of God is just waiting to be revealed to you through the words in the Bible. The Bible is not the only means for discerning God's hidden presence in our lives, but it certainly is *a* way. You don't have to read the Bible, but that's like saying you don't have to read Shakespeare, or listen to John Coltrane, or enjoy the art of Georgia O'Keefe. The Bible is a cultural treasure. Parts of it are maddening, parts of it are so culturally foreign to Westerners of our time as to be virtually indecipherable, but many passages in the Bible are luminous, radiant with wisdom and compassion and the promise of union with a God who is the source of all love and joy. Who wouldn't want that?

* * *

Speaking of love, I'd like to leave you with a little thought experiment. The next time you pick up your Bible, as you read it, mentally substitute the word *Love* for *God*. It's a great way to remind us that the only god worth worshipping is the God who is the source of all true love, compassion, mercy, and justice. It's a great way to circumvent the problems of language, where *God* has too often been used as a code word for a patriarchal, cis/heteronormative authority figure. To read the Bible like a mystic, deconstruct all your old images of God and let the Mystery of Love guide you instead. Embrace the unknowing, consent to the mystery, and trust that you deserve joy (you also deserve to clean up your mess and care for others, but joy makes all that possible, so it comes first). You have a treasure in your heart. I hope when you read the Bible, you will read it through the eyes of that treasure and that it will help you know that treasure more and more.

* * *

APPENDIX
Lectio Divina and Ignatian Prayer

* * *

The wisdom of the scriptures is learned rather by prayer than by study.

—Saint Philip Neri

IN CHAPTER 4, we looked at different approaches to reading the Bible, including the contemplative approach—which I equated to Origen of Alexandria's moral interpretation of the Bible (*moral* not only in the sense of being a good person but also in the broader sense of reading the Bible for personal spiritual growth). In our time, two methods of praying with the Bible have become especially popular: *lectio divina* and Ignatian prayer. I believe these two methods of praying/reading the Bible are the best tools we have for learning to read it like a contemplative, which in turn is a key step toward reading the Bible like a mystic. Many contemplative seekers in our time are already familiar with *lectio divina* and Ignatian prayer, but since they may be new practices for some people, it seems helpful to briefly explain them. Even if you have been using *lectio* or Ignatian practices for many years, hopefully this appendix will be a helpful resource for review.

Lectio Divina

Lectio divina has been a part of Christian spirituality since at least the sixth century and perhaps long before that. It is a beautiful way to integrate four essential practices: engaging with the word of God as encountered in sacred Scripture, meditating on the graces and mysteries of faith, praying as a way of opening the thoughts of our mind and feelings of our heart to God, and resting in the vast open presence of contemplative silence. *Lectio* is an integral spiritual method that effortlessly weaves these four dimensions of devotion into one meaningful daily exercise.

A short treatise called *The Ladder of Monks* written by Guigo II, a twelfth-century Carthusian monk, spells out the basic process for engaging in *lectio divina*. The heart of the practice is not so much what we do (or even the order in which we do it) but the way we approach the text we are reading. Find a passage in the Bible that you would like to read—it can be from either the Hebrew Scriptures or the New Testament, and it need not be very long. Indeed, shorter passages work better for the practice of *lectio*, so if you are reading a long chapter or section of the Bible, consider just reading a portion each time you do *lectio*. Once you select your passage, here are the steps to take in reading it:

- *Lectio* (read)—The key is to read slowly, prayerfully, meditatively. Linger over the words, savoring their message for you. Do not encumber yourself with Bible commentaries or other supplemental books; save those for study time. Rather, take your passage, no matter how brief it is—maybe even just one verse or a few verses—and read it slowly, attentively, mindfully. This is not a race. Read the passage and reread it. You can keep reading until it seems that a particular word or phrase is speaking to you but stop then. Allow a sacred pause. Take a few relaxing breaths. Now you are ready to move on to the next step.

- *Meditatio* (reflect)—Traditionally, meditation as understood within Christian mysticism involved the process of thoughtful reflection on a word, concept, teaching, or what has been called the *mysteries of the faith*. Allow yourself to sit with the word or phrase that has been spoken to you. Feel whatever feeling it elicits in you. Ponder what questions it asks of you. Perhaps you feel blessed, inspired, confused, challenged, or convicted. Simply let this sacred word or words speak to you. At this point, it's less about you reading the Bible and more about the word of God "reading" you. Sooner or later, every conversation involves give and take, so at some point, you'll be ready for the next step.

- *Oratio* (respond)—God reveals Divine Love to us through sacred Scripture, and now we are asked to reveal the hidden depths of our hearts and minds to God through prayer. I suppose it goes without saying that God already knows the hidden places in our hearts and minds, but it is a blessing when we consciously seek to hold those secret dimensions in the light of Love. Pray to God in response to the words you have read and the reflections you have pondered. You don't have to be eloquent or fancy in your prayer. It could be as simple as "God, I love you" or "Holy One, today's reading really confused/upset me." Be honest with God. Express your doubts, longings, desires, fears, or dreams. Express adoration and devotion, of course; confess sins when that is necessary as well. Take however long you need to share your mind and heart with the God who is Love. This doesn't need to last forever (it might only take a minute or two). You'll sense when you have prayed all you need to pray, at least in terms of thoughts and feelings. Then it is time for the final step.

- *Contemplatio* (rest)—"Be still and know that I am God," speaks the divine voice in Psalm 46; in other verses in the Psalms, we are invited to let our souls rest for God in silence and even to recognize that silence itself is praise. We begin the process of *lectio divina* by seeking the word of God through the Bible, and we end by seeking the silence of God through contemplative stillness—the prayer of restful, attentive silence. Here we relax into doing nothing more than breathing gently, allowing our thoughts and feelings to come and go without commentary or attachment. We can use a prayer word or verse (a traditional favorite is "God, come to my assistance; Lord, make haste to help me") as a way of focusing our mind/heart so that we are less likely to be distracted during this period of rest. This is like bringing the concept of the Sabbath into our prayer: we seek to grow in love of God simply by resting in God's heart, the way a small child rests in their mother's lap. We let go and let God. We praise the Spirit simply by resting in silence, trusting in Divine Love to hold us.

To finish the process of *lectio divina*, you might want to write about your experience in a journal; if it was especially moving (or difficult), consider sharing it with a soul friend or spiritual companion for further reflection.

Monks and nuns and other Christians with a lively thirst for God have engaged in this simple prayer practice for centuries, giving some time every day to the adventure of falling ever more deeply in love with God through reading the Bible, reflecting on the Word, responding to God in prayer, and then resting in Divine Love and silence.

Ignatian Prayer

Living at the time of the Reformation, Saint Ignatius of Loyola (1491–1556) was one of the founders of the Society of Jesus (the Jesuits) and the author of the *Spiritual Exercises*, a robust program for sustained prayer and meditation through a thirty-day full-time retreat or part time over eight months or more. Many people experience the spiritual exercises as life-changing. Central to the prayer of the *Spiritual Exercises* is a form of praying using the imagination, which was not original to Ignatius (we know of a medieval Cistercian monk, Aelred of Rievaulx, who taught a very similar method of pray-ing), but it has become so associated with Ignatius's spiritual exercises that *Ignatian prayer* has become a synonym for *prayer using your imagination.* The key—and what makes it relevant to our purposes in this book—is that this kind of imaginative prayer begins with a story from the Bible. Here is how Igna-tius himself describes this method of prayer:

> *It will be profitable with the aid of the imagination to apply the five senses to the subject matter of the [prayer] in the following manner: . . . seeing in imagination the persons, and in contemplating and meditating in detail the circumstances in which they are, and then in drawing some fruit from what has been seen . . . to hear what they are saying, or what they might say, and then by reflecting on oneself to*

draw some profit from what has been heard . . . to
smell the infinite fragrance, and taste the infinite
sweetness of the divinity. Likewise to apply these senses
to the soul and its virtues, and to all according to the
person we are contemplating . . . to apply the sense
of touch, for example, by embracing and kissing the
place where the persons stand or are seated, always
taking care to draw some fruit from this.

In other words, when you read a passage in the Bible about Jesus or one of the apostles or one of the great prophets and heroes of the Hebrew Scriptures, use your imagination to *place yourself* into the story as if you were actually there watching it unfold (Ignatius called this the "composition of place"). Like Ignatius said, use all the "senses" of your imagination: visualize the scene; imagine hearing the sounds, smelling the smells, and so forth. The more vividly you can use your imagination to place yourself into the scene, the better. Once you have placed yourself imaginatively into the scene, watch it unfold the way you would watch an exciting or engaging movie: you might even forget that this is all just happening in your mind's eye.

Naturally, the foundation of Ignatian prayer is to "watch" a Bible scene, as if you were a spectator, as it is described in the text. But you can take it even a step further: you can imagine actually interacting with Jesus or whomever else is in the story (since most Christians traditionally revere Jesus as one with God, let's stick with him). Imagine making eye contact with Jesus, listening to what he has to say, and sharing with him what is on your mind. Notice if he has something to say to you—perhaps a word of advice or encouragement or a question or challenge. Pay attention to what this interaction with Jesus is like for you and what kind of emotional response you might feel in return. Pay special attention if this imaginal encounter fills you with a particularly strong response: perhaps you will feel deep joy or gladness, a sense of grief or sorrow, or even be moved to tears. Resist any urge to judge the experience, although if it leaves you puzzled, you might enjoy sharing it with a soul friend or spiritual companion for further reflection or discernment.

Clearly, Ignatian prayer is more than just a rote reading of the letter of the biblical story. It's a spiritual invitation to use the mythic stories in the Bible as a jumping-off place for igniting your spiritual imagination, seeking that interior encounter with the Spirit of infinite love and compassion. Praying this way not only can help you to become more familiar with the biblical stories but also to deeply explore how those stories can shape your relationship with God, Christ, the Spirit, here and now in the present moment.

*   *   *

Are there parallels between *lectio divina* and Ignatian prayer? Certainly. Both methods of reading/praying Scripture begin with a story from the Bible, an engagement with that story within our own spiritual imagination, leading to a hoped-for experience of encountering God—even if only on the level of the imagination. *Lectio* then culminates with an invitation into contemplative silence, a step that could easily be grafted on to the Ignatian method as well.

These practices for reading the Bible in a contemplative, meditative, and imaginative way may seem odd or exotic if you are only used to a more left-brained study of Scripture. But both of these practices are centuries old and have a long heritage of mystics and contemplatives finding them meaningful ways to encounter God. Keep that in mind and let your imagination soar. Who knows what you and the Spirit, together, will get up to?

* * *

WORDS OF GRATITUDE

THIS BOOK HAS benefited from the wisdom and guidance of two gifted editors. So much gratitude to Lil Copan for mentoring me on the necessary task of articulating the social and political dimensions of the life of faith. I am convinced that contemplative and mystical spirituality, at its heart, is the spirituality of radical justice, equality, inclusivity, and liberation, and Lil has been instrumental in helping me develop my voice with courage and trust in the Spirit. Jarrod Harrison gets a special nod of thanks for inviting me to consider how I have an "ecosystems" approach to the Bible and how my approach to reading it involves a type of "undressing" (a much more delightful metaphor than Michelangelo's chipping away at the marble block!). Jarrod also encouraged me to dive deeper into my contention that fundamentalism and other dualistic ways of reading the Bible are more about power and control than the liberating action of the Spirit.

Thanks to my agent, Linda Roghaar, and the team at Broadleaf Books for inspiration, support, and brainstorming as I developed and wrote this book.

A special word of thanks to Brian D. McLaren, who gave me some helpful ideas and advice when I was first formulating the idea that became this book and especially for his wonderful story about the rabbi on the plane and his presentation at the CAC Emergent Church conference in 2009. Fifteen years later and I'm still talking about that gorilla.

Mark Dannenfelser, Kathy Farrell, Cynthia Hizer, Cindy Howard, Rosary Mangano, Linda Mitchell, Debonee Morgan, Margaret Putnam, David Rensberger, Kay Satterfield, Fr. Thomas Francis Smith, OCSO, Rick Tyler, and Gareth Young are some of the wonderful friends and associates who have been dialogue partners, sounding boards, and just plain fun people to hang out with as I've developed the ideas in this book. If I'm leaving anyone out, my apologies.

Love, as always, to Fran, my spouse, best friend, travel buddy, and ongoing co-adventurer as I journey through the process of writing and the even more vital and beautiful process of simply living. You continue to surprise, delight, and amaze me. It's a joy to share life with you.

Portions of this book originally appeared, in slightly different form in my blog, *Anamchara*, found at www.anamchara.com (check it out). Other portions originally appeared on Patreon (www.patreon.com/carlmccolman); check that out too. As always, profound gratitude to the many people who support my work as a writer through Patreon. Your generosity and encouragement literally keep me going.

And a final note, but certainly not an afterthought: this book was written on Mvskoke (Muscogee) land.

Carl McColman
Trinity Sunday 2024

NOTES

Epigraph

ix   ***"For one word of [the Bible] will contain":*** Teresa of Ávila, "Meditations on the Song of Songs," 1.2, in *Collected Works of St. Teresa of Avila* (Washington, DC: ICS Publications, 2012), 2:284–285, Kindle. Edited for the sake of inclusive language. Teresa herself wrote, "For one word of His will contain within itself a thousand mysteries." The context of this quotation makes it clear that Teresa is referring to the Bible, which she understood to be "the word of God"—and as was customary for her time, she referred to God using masculine pronouns.

Chapter 1: Michelangelo's Statue

1   ***"Whether it's the Bible or the Qur'an":*** Brian C. Muraresku, *The Immortality Key* (New York: St. Martin's, 2020), Introduction, Kindle.

4   ***"If a thing is worth doing . . .":*** G. K. Chesterton, "What's Wrong with the World," Project Gutenberg, pt. 4, chap. 14, December 9, 2008, last updated October 2016, last accessed October 15, 2024, https:// www.gutenberg .org/files/1717/1717-h/1717-h.htm #link2H_4_0045.

9   ***Nowadays, you can find many different commentaries:*** Carol A. Newsom, Sharon H. Ringe, and Jacqueline E. Lapsley, eds., *Women's Bible Commentary, Revised*

and Updated, 3rd ed. (Louisville, KY: Westminster John Knox Press, 2012); Mona West and Robert E. Shore-Goss, eds., *The Queer Bible Commentary,* 2nd ed. (London: SCM Press, 2022).

10 *If you are new to mysticism:* Carl McColman, *The New Big Book of Christian Mysticism* (Minneapolis: Broadleaf Books, 2023); Evelyn Underhill, *Mysticism: A Study in the Nature and Development of Human Consciousness,* 12th ed. (Mineola, NY: Dover Publications, 2002); John Mabry, *Growing into God: A Beginner's Guide to Christian Mysticism* (Wheaton, IL: Quest Books, 2012).

10 *The great German theologian Karl Rahner famously said:* Karl Rahner, *Concern for the Church* (NewYork: Crossroad, 1981), 149.

11 *Wonderful books on those foundational spiritual practices:* Michael Casey, *Sacred Reading: The Ancient Art of Lectio Divina* (Liguori, MO: Triumph Books, 1996); Christine Valters Paintner, *Lectio Divina, The Sacred Art: Transforming Words & Images Into Heart-Centered Prayer* (Woodstock, VT: Skylight Paths, 2011); Margaret Silf, *Inner Compass: An Invitation to Ignatian Spirituality* (Chicago: Loyola Press, 2007); Timothy Gallagher, *An Ignatian Introduction to Prayer* (New York: Crossroad, 2007).

12 *"Holy Scripture containeth all things":* This quotation comes from the Articles of Religion of the Episcopal Church, found in *The Book of Common Prayer* (New York: Church Hymnal Corporation, 1979), 868.

13 *Famous Zen teacher:* Shunryu Suzuki, *Zen Mind, Beginner's Mind: Informal Talks on Zen Meditation and Practice* (New York: Weatherhill, 1970), 21.

Chapter 2: Can the Bible Be Saved?

15 *"I asked [my grandmother] one day"*: Howard Thurman, *Jesus and the Disinherited* (Beacon Press, 2022), chap. 1, Kindle.

31 *According to a recent poll conducted by the Pew Research Center:* The Pew Research Center's findings on the prevalence of biblical fundamentalism can be accessed at www .pewresearch.org/religious-landscape-study/database /interpreting-scripture/, last accessed October 15, 2024.

31 *"Mysticism is the antidote to fundamentalism"*: Rick Doblin quoted in Michael Pollan, *How to Change Your Mind* (New York: Penguin Publishing Group, 2018), chap. 1, Kindle.

33 *"Without a doubt, I fear those who fear the devil"*: Teresa of Ávila, *The Book of My Life*, trans. Mirabai Starr (Shambhala, 2011), pt. 3, chap. XXV, Kindle.

Chapter 3: Reclaiming the Mystical Heart of Scripture

37 *"Underneath all the moralizing and polemic"*: Maggie Ross, *Silence: A User's Guide, Volume Two: Application* (Eugene, OR: Cascade Books, 2018), chap. 3, Kindle.

40 *When I first learned about Christian mysticism:* Underhill, *Mysticism.*

42 *he had us watch a video featuring a group of basketball players:* The basketball video with the gorilla was produced by Christopher Chabris and Daniel Simons. To learn more about their work, visit www.theinvisible-gorilla.com.

44 *"The nature of a word is to reveal"*: Meister Eckhart, *The Complete Mystical Works of Meister Eckhart*, trans. Maurice O'C Walshe (New York: Herder and Herder, 2009), 34–35.

45 *"Each article of faith refers to reality"*: John O'Donnell, *A Faith You Can Live With* (Lanham, MD: Sheed and Ward, 1999), 13.

Chapter 4: Four Approaches to the Bible

49 *"Individuals ought to portray the ideas"*: Origen of Alexandria, *On First Principles*, bk. 4, ch. 1, sec. 11. My translation.

61 *"Consequently, there is no such thing as **the one correct interpretation"***: Sandra Schneiders, *The Revelatory Text* (San Francisco: Harper, 1991), 153.

Chapter 5: Miracles, Myth, and Imagination

71 *"Imagination is your interior sense"*: Thomas Merton, *"God Speaks to Each of Us": The Poetry and Letters of Rainer Maria Rilke*, audio recording made on November 14, 1965, Now You Know Media.

Chapter 6: Guidance from the Mystics

83 *"If you would grasp Christ"*: Bernard of Clairvaux, *The Letters of Bernard of Clairvaux*, trans. Bruno Scott James (Kalamazoo, MI: Cistercian Publications, 1998), letter 107, 156.

88 *the names of God are to be learned from Scripture only:* "The Catholic Encyclopedia," last accessed October 15, 2024, Pseudo-Dionysius, www.newadvent.org/cathen/05013a.htm.

89   *So when one person has said "Moses thought what I
      say,"*: Saint Augustine, *The Confessions*, trans. Henry Chad-
      wick (Oxford: Oxford World's Classics, 2009), 270–271.

90   *Hildegard of Bingen described herself:* Carmen Ace-
      vedo Butcher, trans., *Hildegard of Bingen: A Spiritual
      Reader* (Brewster, MA: Paraclete Press, 2007), 121.

90   *"tells how in 1141 she received 'a fiery light of exceed-
      ing brilliance'"*: Bernard McGinn, *The Presence of God,
      Volume 2: The Growth of Mysticism* (New York: Crossroad
      Publishing, 1994), 336.

92   *Julian remarks that her visions gave her a new per-
      spective:* Julian of Norwich, *The Complete Julian of Nor-
      wich*, ed. Fr. John Julian (Brewster, MA: Paraclete Press,
      2012), chaps. 48, 49, Kindle. Language adapted slightly
      to make it more inclusive.

92   *For wrath is nothing else but a rebellion:* Julian of Nor-
      wich, *The Complete Julian of Norwich*.

94   *Julian very simply states:* Julian of Norwich, *The Com-
      plete Julian of Norwich*.

95   *Julian reasonably argues:* Julian of Norwich, *The Com-
      plete Julian of Norwich*.

100   *"Our concern is not with the historical accuracy":* Pauli
      Murray, "Out of the Wilderness," in *To Speak a Defiant Word*
      (New Haven, CT: Yale University Press, 2023), Kindle.

101   *His biographer Michael Battle highlights Tutu's mys-
      ticism:* Michael Battle, *Desmond Tutu: A Spiritual
      Biography of South Africa's Confessor* (Louisville, KY:
      Westminster John Knox Press, 2021).

101   *"We must be ready to learn from one another":* Des-
      mond Tutu, *God Is Not a Christian* (San Francisco:
      Harper, 2011), chap. 1, Kindle.

103   *that the consciousness we bring to the Bible:* Richard
      Rohr, *What Do We Do with the Bible?* (Albuquerque,

NM: CAC Publishing, 2018), 20–21. See also Rohr, *Things Hidden: Scripture as Spirituality* (Cincinnati: St. Anthony Messenger Press, 2008).

Chapter 7: Purification, Illumination, Union, and Beyond

105 *"But as the study of physical life":* Evelyn Underhill, *Mysticism: A Study in the Nature and Development of Spiritual Consciousness* (Mineola, NY: Dover Publications, 2012), pt. 2, chap. 1, Kindle.

110 *"fearless moral inventory":* This phrase comes from step four of the Twelve-Step Program, in which a person who is recovering from an addiction undertakes a "fearless moral inventory" to be conscious of all the actions they have done that have caused harm to others. This is followed by a process of making amends as appropriate and seeking spiritual help to change their lives for the better. See *The Big Book: 12 Steps and 12 Traditions* (New York: Alcoholics Anonymous World Services, 2001), The Twelve Steps, Kindle.

114 *"Christian life consists not so much in being good":* Michael Casey, *Fully Human, Fully Divine: An Interactive Christology* (Liguori, MO: Liguori Publications, 2004), Preface, Kindle.

115 *dark night of the self:* See Cynthia Bourgeault, *Thomas Keating: The Making of a Modern Christian Mystic* (Boston: Shambhala, 2024).

117 *"A map is not the territory it represents":* Alfred Korzybski, *Science and Sanity: An Introduction to Non-Aristotelian Systems and General Semantics* (New York: International Non-Aristotelian Library Publishing Company, 1933), 58.

127 ***bear Christ into the world:*** Caryll Houselander, *The Reed of God: A New Edition of a Spiritual Classic* (Notre Dame, IN: Christian Classics, 2006), Introduction, Kindle.

134 ***everything belongs:*** The title of one of Richard Rohr's books, "Everything Belongs" is his way of describing the nondual experience of contemplative prayer. See Richard Rohr, *Everything Belongs: The Gift of Contemplative Prayer* (New York: Crossroad, 2003).

Chapter 8: Seven Keys to Unlock the Bible

139 ***"The mysteries of the faith":*** Simone Weil, *Awaiting God* (Abbotsford, BC: Fresh Wind Press, 2012), Letter to a Priest, #26, Kindle.

Chapter 9: Scripture and Spiritual Transformation

155 ***"To think of oneself as a child of God":*** Pauli Murray, *To Speak a Defiant Word* (New Haven, CT: Yale University Press, 2023), Father's Day Sermon, Kindle.

157 ***"The man who never alters his opinion":*** William Blake, "The Marriage of Heaven and Hell," plate 19, in *William Blake: The Complete Illuminated Books* (New York: Thames & Hudson, 2000), p. 125. See *The Complete Poetry and Prose of William Blake*, ed. David V. Erdman (Oakland: University of California Press, 2008), 42.

159 ***people who live in sustained periods of solitude:*** Regarding solitary confinement, see www.scientificamerican.com/article/solitary-confinement-cruel-ineffective-unusual/.

168 ***In some He is newly born:*** Caryll Houselander, *The Reed of God: A New Edition of a Spiritual Classic* (Notre Dame, IN: Christian Classics, 2020), The Way, Kindle.

Chapter 10: Read the Bible like a Mystic

173 *Wise people know their wisdom is not self-generated:* Rohr, *What Do We Do with the Bible?*, 20–21.

Appendix: *Lectio Divina* and Ignatian Prayer

183 *"The wisdom of the scriptures":* St. Philip Neri, *Maxims and Sayings of St. Philip Neri*, accessed October 15, 2024, www.liturgialatina.org/oratorian/maxims.htm.

189 *It will be profitable with the aid of the imagination:* St. Ignatius of Loyola, *The Spiritual Exercises of St. Ignatius: Based on Studies in the Language of the Autograph*, trans. Louis J. Puhl, SJ (Chicago: Loyola Press, 1951), The Fifth Contemplation, paras. 121–125, Kindle.